ILLUSTRATED TALES OF
SUFFOLK

JOHN LING

AMBERLEY

Acknowledgements

The author would like to thank the following for their valued assistance:

John and Rosalind Middleton and family; Adrian Cable; Keith Evans; Roger Jones; Sylvia Le Comber; Bungay Castle Trust; Dunwich Greyfriars Trust; Friends of St Mary's Church, Bungay.

First published 2020

Amberley Publishing
The Hill, Stroud
Gloucestershire, GL5 4EP

www.amberley-books.com

British Library Cataloguing in Publication Data.
A catalogue record for this book is available from the British Library.

ISBN 978 1 3981 0099 2 (paperback)
ISBN 978 1 3981 0100 5 (ebook)

Origination by Amberley Publishing.
Printed in Great Britain.

Contents

Introduction   4

The Black Dog of Bungay and Other Tales   5

The Green Children and Other Strange Stories   12

Tales from the Suffolk Coast   22

Legends of Edmund: King, Martyr and Saint   37

Anne Boleyn's Heart and Other Stories   42

Maria Marten and the Red Barn Murder   50

More Mysterious Murders   55

Suffolk Witchcraft Trials   65

Church and Churchyard Tales   72

Haunted Hostelries   80

Modern Tales: Atomic Bombs, UFOs and a 'Timeslip'   86

Bibliography   96

Introduction

The historic county of Suffolk has more than its fair share of strange tales. From ancient legends, through stories of the supernatural to more modern documented cases, there is much to tell. *Illustrated Tales of Suffolk* brings together many different kinds of stories from around the county, including folklore, witchcraft, murder, smuggling and much besides.

Where possible I have tried to include obscure or lesser-known tales, though inevitably, a number will have appeared in print before. One of Suffolk's best supernatural tales is that of the Black Dog of Bungay, closely related to the dreaded Black Shuck which is reputed to have haunted much of East Anglia and beyond for up to a thousand years. Another odd story relates to the Green Children of Woolpit, a brother and sister with green-tinged skin, neither of whom could speak English, who were found in a wolf pit during the twelfth century. Several old tales are linked with the Suffolk coast including the Wild Man of Orford, who was captured in nets and imprisoned in the castle, and Suffolk's answer to 'Nessie', the mysterious Kessingland Sea Serpent. The submerged city of Dunwich, often dubbed 'Britain's Atlantis', has also spawned strange legends.

Several of Suffolk's historical characters have fascinating tales to tell, but there are often conflicting versions of events and the line between fact and fiction can easily become blurred. Some real-life stories have acquired a sub-plot of intrigue or conspiracy and others have paranormal elements attached to them. Many tales have been told of St Edmund, the ninth-century King of East Anglia who gave his name to Bury St Edmunds. Another royal connection relates to the casket found in a Suffolk church which according to legend contained the heart of Queen Anne Boleyn. The 'Red Barn' murder of Maria Marten in Polstead in 1827 is also included, along with other Suffolk murders. Other interesting characters include the Newbourne Giants, two brothers who stood 7 feet 7 inches (2.32 metres) and 7 feet 4 inches (2.23 metres) tall respectively. George Orwell, the influential author of *1984* and *Animal Farm*, wrote some of his earlier works while living in Suffolk, and also reported an encounter with a phantom figure in a ruined church.

More modern stories include the mysteries of Orford Ness, where until relatively recently top-secret military tests were carried out, and the Rendlesham Forest UFO incident of 1980 which some have called 'Britain's Roswell'. An alleged wartime invasion attempt and an unexplained 'timeslip' are also featured.

The Black Dog of Bungay and Other Tales

As a child I first heard the Black Dog of Bungay legend from my father, who was born and raised in the small market town. Though similar to the Black Shuck tales well known throughout East Anglia, this story differs in that it is specific to particular locations. Like Black Shuck, Bungay's Black Dog is believed to be a giant supernatural hound that has been sighted on many occasions over the centuries. Its most infamous appearance was in the late sixteenth century, but tales of black dogs in Bungay go back much further in time.

The first reports of black dog sightings in the town are connected with Bungay Castle, originally built in the early twelfth century by Roger Bigod (*c.* 1060–1107) and rebuilt by his son Hugh (*c.* 1095–1176) in 1165, a year after it was returned to the Bigod family by King Henry II who had earlier taken it from them. Hugh Bigod acquired a fearsome reputation as a ruthless and evil man, and following

Bigod's castle, Bungay.

his death in Palestine during a crusade, stories began to circulate that a huge black dog was haunting Bungay Castle. This was believed by the townsfolk to be the restless Hugh in supernatural canine form. A boy who witnessed the manifestation was said to have dropped down dead on the spot and the castle became a place to avoid after the sun had gone down.

By far the most significant date in the legend of the Black Dog was 4 August 1577. Being a Sunday, the good people of Bungay were gathered in St Mary's Church during a severe storm when an enormous hound burst into the building and killed two members of the terrified congregation and severely injured another. After wreaking havoc in Bungay, the creature re-materialised around 12 miles away at Holy Trinity Church, Blythburgh. Here it created further chaos, attacking and slaying two more men and a boy before rushing out of the church. As the beast ran down the aisle of Blythburgh Church, the steeple came crashing down through the nave roof. Marks on the inside of the north door, allegedly made either by its claws or red-hot breath while trying to escape, can still be seen to this day. Similar marks were apparently left on the door of St Mary's Church, but the great fire that destroyed much of Bungay on 1 March 1688 obliterated all trace. Some accounts state that the Black Dog visited Blythburgh Church first, while others ignore the events in Bungay and attribute the Blythburgh incident to Black Shuck.

Much of the Black Dog of Bungay tale can be traced back to a pamphlet written by the Revd Abraham Fleming, who was Rector of St Pancras Church

St Mary's Church and Priory ruins, Bungay.

in London and also an author and editor. His pamphlet, *A Straunge and Terrible Wunder wrought in the Parish Church of St Mary*, was first published soon after the event. In it he vividly describes how three men were attacked in the church but one survived his injuries despite being 'drawn together and shrunk up as it were a piece of leather scorched in a hot fire'. Fleming described the demon dog as 'the divel (sic) in such a likeness'. A reprint of his pamphlet from 1826 includes a poem from which the following verses are taken:

> The church appear'd a mass of flame
> And while the storm did rage
> A black and fearful monster came
> All eyes he did engage.
> All down the church in midst of fire
> The Hellish monster flew
> And passing onward to the quire
> He many people slew.
>
> Many were stricken to the ground
> Whereof they strangely died
> And many others there were found
> Wounded on every side.
> The church itself was rent and torn
> The clock in pieces broke
> Two men who in the belfry sat
> Were killed upon the spot.

Abraham Fleming probably never set foot in Bungay, so his account is presumably based on reports from afar. The official church record states that two men in the belfry died after being struck by lightning, and names them as Adam Walker and John Fuller. According to an entry in the Churchwardens' Register two years later, there were other casualties during the storm. It reports that some parishioners were 'stryken down to the ground and some hurt in diverse places of their legs and feet'. No reference was made to the involvement of a dog.

Some believe that the superstitious townsfolk interpreted the appalling weather conditions as the Devil's work and that the infamous hound was simply a mass hallucination. This seems rather harsh on Bungay's citizens, many of whom no doubt worked on the land and would have been familiar with all manner of weather phenomena including thunder and lightning. They would not have been unduly alarmed by a severe storm, though if the lightning had found its way from the belfry into the packed church it would inevitably have caused much fear and panic among the congregation. It is recorded that the town had problems with stray dogs, so it is not beyond the realms of possibility

Black Dog weathervane, Bungay.

that during the ensuing pandemonium one could have sought refuge from the storm and attacked some of the parishioners. In any event, the story has been handed down the centuries and is now firmly established in Bungay folklore. The fabled beast tops a weathervane in the town centre and the local football team are nicknamed the 'Black Dogs'.

On one visit to St Mary's Church, I found many drawings of the Black Dog by local schoolchildren and discovered that I had inadvertently arrived on 4 August, the anniversary of its fateful appearance. I was about to leave when I distinctly heard a single howl which stopped me in my tracks. The culprit was surely one of the flesh and blood canines walking with their owners on the footpath through the churchyard, but it felt slightly spooky all the same! The ruins of St Mary's Priory in the churchyard are reputedly still occasionally visited by the Black Dog, and the eerie sounds of monks chanting, women singing and phantom bells ringing have all been heard.

I have also examined the marks on the north door of Blythburgh Church, though who or what made them is open to debate. A new village sign featuring the so-called 'Angel of the East' has stood guard outside the church since the summer of 2000. Perhaps she is looking out for another visitation from the dreaded Black Dog?

Holy Trinity Church, Blythburgh.

Successful novelist Sir Henry Rider Haggard, who lived at Ditchingham near Bungay, mentioned the legend in his non-fiction work *A Farmer's Year* (1898) and was said to have actually seen the beast. In his *The Supernatural Coast*, Peter Haining describes in detail another local man's eerie encounter one autumn evening in 1938. In brief, the man claimed that a large dog with 'a long, black, shaggy coat' was approaching from the opposite direction as he was making his way home to Ditchingham. As it drew level with the witness the dog suddenly disappeared! The same author also relates a tale from the early twentieth century of a sighting in Leiston churchyard. Two women, one of whom he identifies as Lady Rendlesham, laid in wait hoping to see a phantom hound rumoured to haunt the area. The creature duly appeared at midnight and the women, who were shaken but unharmed, were convinced that they had seen something otherworldly.

These stories bear more resemblance to the traditional Black Shuck legend than to the events of 1577. The Black Dog of Bungay tale stands alone in its description of violent attacks inside two packed churches during thunderstorms on the same day. Most alleged sightings of Black Shuck take place in secluded locations, often but by no means exclusively close to the coast after dark. It is sometimes said to have a single huge eye in the centre of its forehead but is more often described as having two glowing red eyes. Large black dogs have also been reported at Aldeburgh, Dunwich, Lowestoft, Southwold and Walberswick. In Aldeborough, Black Shuck is said to roam a secluded lane and will silently walk beside you as long as you travel in the same direction as he does. If you try to go in the opposite direction he will bar your way and growl loudly until you turn around. A coastguard at Walberswick reportedly fired his gun at the legendary beast during the Second World War but it simply disappeared. The inland village of Wissett, near Halesworth, has two bridges on Mill Lane where Black Shuck is said to materialise.

Phantom white dogs have also been seen and in some areas are known as Gally Trots or White Shuck. In Burgh near Woodbridge, tales of a huge white dog have circulated for centuries. It is said to protect St Botolph's churchyard from evil intruders, but also wanders along local lanes and further afield. A strange haunting specific to Walberswick Common relates to a white dog resembling an

Above left: North door, Holy Trinity Church, Blythburgh; *Above right*: Blythburgh village sign.

oversized pointer. It has been reported intermittently since the nineteenth century and is said to lie down in the undergrowth. When approached it gets up and silently trots away. This entity is entirely separate from the Black Shuck encounter at Walberswick described above.

An intriguing postscript to these stories was reported by local and national newspapers in May 2014, following the discovery of a huge dog's skeleton at the ruined Leiston Abbey during an archaeological dig. The articles claimed that the animal would have stood 7 feet (2.13 metres) tall on its hind legs and weighed in excess of 14 stone. The media immediately linked the astonishing find with the Black Shuck legend, prompting speculation that these could actually be the bones of the notorious 'hellhound'. The story was covered on an episode of *The One Show* (BBC TV) in October 2014, which revealed that carbon dating tests on the skeleton indicated a probable date of between 1794 and 1854. The animal, possibly a Great Dane kept as a guard or hunting dog, may have been a frightening sight particularly after dark. Could it account for some of the Black Shuck reports in the general area around that time?

The Black Shuck legend is believed to have inspired Sir Arthur Conon Doyle's *The Hound of the Baskervilles*, often rated as the best of the Sherlock Holmes stories. More recently, Lowestoft heavy rock band The Darkness included a track called *Black Shuck* on their 2003 album *Permission to Land*, rhyming the demon dog's name with a word that I won't repeat here!

The Green Children and Other Strange Stories

The Green Children of Woolpit

One of Suffolk's oddest and most baffling legends is that of the Green Children of Woolpit, a village near Bury St Edmunds. Its name refers not to wool but to the pits in which wolves were trapped in Saxon times. In one such pit, locals discovered a boy and a girl said to be green in colour who could speak no English. They were offered various foodstuffs including bread at Wikes Hall near Bardwell, the residence of Sir Richard de Calne, but it was only when they spied newly gathered green beans that they began to eat. For a while they refused all other food but gradually accepted a more varied diet 'and they lost completely their green colour'. The girl worked for Sir Richard for several years before marrying a King's Lynn man and later gave birth to a number of children of both sexes. Her brother, however, had been in poor health since his discovery and 'died within a short time'.

Much of the written information regarding the Green Children comes from Ralph of Coggeshall, an abbot of a Cistercian monastery in Essex, who died

Woolpit village sign.

around 1228. Another account was written by William of Newburgh (1136–98), a canon of an Augustinian priory in Yorkshire. The children were found either during the reign of King Stephen (1135–54) or King Henry II (1154–89). One of many mysterious elements of this tale is, of course, the fact that the siblings were described as being green. If the village sign is to be believed they were green from head to toe, though Ralph of Coggeshall, who was rumoured to have learned the story first hand from Sir Richard de Calne, described their skin colour as 'tinged with green'. William of Newburgh may have exaggerated this aspect of their appearance. Perhaps the main clue is that they apparently lost this green hue when they accepted other food. It is therefore likely that they originally had sallow complexions that gradually disappeared when their diet improved. Some seem to have taken the Green Children description a little too literally, suggesting that they may have been extraterrestrials left behind when their spaceship took off without them! Others dismiss the whole thing as fantasy and doubt that the pair ever existed. It seems unlikely that such an

Woolpit Church.

unusual tale would not have some factual basis and it is said that descendents of the girl were still living in or around King's Lynn during at least the first half of the twentieth century.

After learning to speak good English, the girl claimed that the pair came from St Martin's Land, an underground world where the sun never shone. A place just north of Bury called Fornham St Martin may be significant, but like most aspects of the tale this is pure conjecture. It is believed that a number of Flemish immigrants were killed around Bury St Edmunds in 1173 during a period of widespread persecution. Could the Green Children have been orphaned during this slaughter? The legend is still alive and well in Woolpit and continues to attract visitors to the village.

Malekin of Dagworth Hall

The strange story of Malekin was another tale recorded by Ralph of Coggeshall and relates to a mysterious entity said to communicate with the residents of Dagworth Hall near Stowmarket. Long absorbed into Suffolk folklore, it seems to have all the hallmarks of a rather sinister haunting. In Ralph's own words it goes as follows:

In the time of King Richard (1189-99), there appeared frequently, and for a long space of time, in the house of Sir Osberni de Bradwelle, at Daghewurthe in Suffolk, a certain fantastical spirit who conversed with the family of the aforesaid knight, always imitating the voice of a one-year-old child. He called himself Malekin, and said that his mother and brother dwelt in a neighbouring house, and that they often chided him because he left them and went to speak with people.

The things which he did and said were both wonderful and very funny and he often told people's secrets. At first the family of the knight were extremely terrified, but by degrees they became used to his words and silly actions, and conversed familiarly with him. He sometimes spoke English, in the dialect of the region, and sometimes in Latin, and he discussed the Scriptures with the chaplain of that same knight, just as he truly testifies to us.

He could be heard and felt too, but not seen, except once as a very small child clothed in a white tunic, in the chamber of a certain maiden. She had asked him to show himself to her, but he would not agree to this request until she swore by God that she would not touch or hold him. He also said that he was born at Lavenham and that his mother had left him in part of a field where she was harvesting and that he had been taken away. He said that he had been in his present position seven years, and that after another seven years he should be restored to his former state of living with people. He said that he and the others had a sort of hat that made him invisible. He often asked for food and drink, which, when placed on a certain chest, immediately disappeared.'

Houses in Lavenham.

Malekin is sometimes referred to as a fairy child or 'changeling', but he claimed to have been abducted from the village of Lavenham while his mother's back was turned. So, who or what was he? If the tale is to be believed, he was capable of intellectual discussion in two languages, yet his only appearance was in the guise of a tiny child. Ralph of Coggeshall describes Malekin as a 'fantastical spirit' and modern writers have speculated that he may have been a poltergeist. It is known that during the 1190s Dagworth Hall was occupied by Sir Osbert Fitzhervey, his wife Margaret and family. There is no record of Malekin after this point.

Dagworth Hall still exists but has long been divided into separate private apartments and much of the present building dates from the fifteenth century. As a footnote to this enthralling but rather perplexing tale, there is an unsubstantiated claim that poltergeist activity during the 1960s led to the swift departure of a tenant living in the oldest part of the house.

The Vanishing Pipers of Beccles

A peculiar old story rather reminiscent of the Pied Piper of Hamelin legend – though thankfully without the missing children element – is attached to the town of Beccles, not far from the border with Norfolk. It is said that three men were once offered a total of 45,000 marks by the portreeve of the local council to rid the town of its enormous rat population. The trio accepted the task and used enchanted pipes or whistles to create magical music that charmed the creatures out from their lairs. The rats followed the men out of the town and into the River Waveney, where they drowned. The townspeople were delighted and very grateful to the pipers but, like the rats, they were never seen again and the money went unclaimed.

It was rumoured in the town that the three men had consulted local 'cunning women' or witches Fanny Barton, Nancy Driver and Sally Price, who lived on the marshes just outside Beccles. One version of the tale says that the men offered the witches one mark each for helping them drive out the vermin, which does not seem particularly generous when they were due to pocket 15,000 marks each. Nevertheless, the women accepted the offer on the condition that the men signed their souls over to the Devil, which is why they never returned to claim their earnings. The portreeve later found that three marks had mysteriously gone missing, despite the money being closely guarded. The witches were suspected but they said nothing and the townsfolk wisely decided that it was safer not to incur their wrath.

The River Waveney at Beccles.

Above left: Beccles town sign; *Above right*: Beccles Church bell tower.

In his *Haunted Suffolk*, author Pete Jennings gives the names of the three pipers as Sam Partridge, a peddler, candle-maker Jonathan Betts, and Peter Harris. He states that 'the town had a Portreeve rather than a Mayor from 1584-1835', though another source claims that the events took place much earlier in 1349. In the years following their disappearance it was said that mysterious music could be heard by the banks of the River Waveney on 31 August, and that three phantom pipers had been seen. Whether their presence is still detected in the area is uncertain.

The Riddle of Freston Tower

Standing by the River Orwell south of Ipswich, the impressive six-storey Freston Tower is something of an enigma and the true reason for its existence is still debated. A well-known tale claims that it was built by a Lord de Freston for the education of his only daughter Ellen. Apparently, the poor girl worked her way up from the ground floor to the summit every day, studying a different subject on each level. Her busy schedule was as follows:

The Lower Room to charity from 7 to 8 o'clock
The Second to tapestry-working from 9 to 10
The Third to music from 10 to noon
The Fourth to painting from 12 to 1
The Fifth to literature from 1 to 2
The Sixth to astronomy at even.

Freston Tower. (Courtesy of Jsc83)

Working such long days on her own it is hardly surprising that Ellen grew tired of this dull routine and eloped with her art master! When Lord de Freston realised what had happened he was beside himself with rage, and some say that his ghost can still be heard some evenings angrily calling for his daughter's return.

This all makes for a good yarn but it is claimed that the whole story was invented by the Revd Richard Cobbold for his novel *Freston Tower* (1850), in which he stated that the building was erected in the fifteenth century and 'was frequently visited by Wolsey as a boy'. In a paper also titled *Freston Tower* (1856), Samuel Tymms rejected most aspects of Cobbold's story including the date and the alleged connection with Cardinal Wolsey. Tymms thought that 'the tower was built by Edmund Latymer, about the year 1549, as a quiet retreat or "pleasaunce tower", for the better enjoyment of the extensive and charming views which are to be obtained from it.'

Various other possible dates of the tower's construction, ranging from around 1557 to 1655, have been quoted by other sources. According to present owners the Landmark Trust, it was probably built as a lookout tower around 1578/9 by 'a wealthy Ipswich merchant called Thomas Gooding who bought Freston Manor in 1553.' They suggest that 'it may even have been built to coincide with Queen Elizabeth's visit to Ipswich in 1579.'

From 1772 to 1779 the tower was used by Mr Buck, an Ipswich surgeon, for the treatment of smallpox patients. It is now available to let as a high-rise holiday location. Whoever built Freston Tower and for whatever reason, it remains a local landmark and has been described as 'arguably the oldest folly in England'.

Tales of Mythical Creatures

In addition to encounters with demonic dogs, Suffolk folklore brims with strange stories of mythical creatures.

The wild man or woodwose was believed to be covered with hair, possess great strength and pick fights with lions and dragons. He lived in woods or forests and was partial to the occasional human child as a supplement to his diet. Club-bearing wild men were often depicted on or inside churches to provide protection against demons and other malevolent entities, and many Suffolk churches still have such carvings. Orford Church's font is decorated with several images of the creatures, and a legend has been passed down the centuries of a medieval wild man who was captured in fishing nets and held captive in Orford Castle. Although he fits the general physical description of the traditional woodwose, he does not conform to the wood or forest dwelling criteria and has his own unique place in Suffolk folklore. The story of the Wild Man of Orford is told in the following chapter, along with tales of other sea 'monsters'.

A woodwose and a wyvern (a two-legged dragon) confront each other above the fifteenth-century porch of Peasenhall Church, but in addition to battles with wild men, dragons also fought members of their own kind. A legend states that a pair of enormous dragons, one from Suffolk and another from Essex, clashed at Little Cornard, almost on the border between the two counties. The two

A wyvern (*above left*) and a woodwose (*above right*), St Michael's Church, Peasenhall.

great beasts battled for an hour watched by many witnesses. The Essex dragon is claimed to have emerged triumphant, but both lived to fight another day. According to a book held at Canterbury Cathedral, the conflict happened on 26 September 1449. Another dragon caused havoc in Bures in 1405, killing and eating sheep and possibly a shepherd as well. The beast was pursued by archers and swam away towards Wormingford, where according to one account it was killed by the townsfolk. A huge etching of the Bures Dragon was created on a hill in 2012 and a fifteenth-century painting can still be viewed in Wissington Church near Nayland. Some believe the creature was a crocodile given to King Richard I by King Saladin, which escaped from the Tower of London, though this appears to have happened two centuries before the events in Bures.

Like neighbouring Norfolk, Suffolk has a strong mermaid tradition but differs in that most of the tales relate to inland areas rather than the seaside. Suffolk mermaids were believed to inhabit ponds, rivers and wells, and pose a threat to humans who went too close to the edge. Children in particular were susceptible to being dragged into the water by the mermaid's long-handled rake or 'crome'. The so-called 'Mermaid Pits' at Fornham All Saints' near Bury St Edmunds were said to be haunted by the spirit of a young lady who drowned herself there centuries ago. Also in Fornham All Saints', a well was alleged to contain a mermaid intent on luring children to their doom, as was a pond in Cottage Wood, Rendlesham. According to John Gage, writing in the early nineteenth century, several mermaids or water sprites distracted workmen constructing a watermill on the River Lark at Hengrave.

A Suffolk mermaid, All Saints' Church, Ringsfield.

Suffolk is famous for its fairy tales, literally relating to the belief in tiny winged creatures, but many of the stories are dark and portray fairies as scary and dangerous. A 'Magic Dell' in a wood at Elveden near Thetford, where a young girl in the nineteenth century heard enchanting music and high-pitched laughter, was thought to be a place where travellers could be captured by the fairy folk. Until relatively recent times, it was widely believed in parts of Suffolk that fairies often stole human babies and left a sickly fairy child or 'changeling' in its place. In his *The History of Stowmarket* (1844) the Revd Arthur Hollingsworth included several tales of local people's encounters with fairies. An elderly woman claimed that her mother awoke one night to find them attempting to steal her baby at the foot of the bed but managed to retrieve it just in time. The woman was unsure whether the child was herself or her sister. Several fairies regularly visited the home of a man and even brought wood for his oven, but after he spoke about it they never returned. Another man, who lived on Bury Road, swore that in 1822 he had seen around twelve fairies dancing silently in a field and described them as being 'light and shadowy, not like solid bodies'. He insisted that he was sober at the time but when he returned with companions the little folk had gone!

Tales from the Suffolk Coast

As might be expected, the Suffolk coast has spawned many strange and interesting tales over the centuries. From the almost fabled underwater city of Dunwich to reports of unexplained sea creatures, the North Sea holds many secrets. Smuggling was once rife along much of the Suffolk coast, either directly or indirectly affecting the lives of numerous citizens.

Drowned Dunwich: Britain's Atlantis?

The lost city of Dunwich gradually disappeared beneath the waves over the course of several centuries, until only isolated fragments remained. Ancient Dunwich had eight churches, three monasteries, two hospitals, its own mint and two seats in parliament. A legend states that church bells can be heard ringing under the sea. Modern visitors still strain to hear the muffled sound of bells that once called the medieval faithful to prayer.

Dunwich was the early capital city of East Anglia and the original seat of the Anglo-Saxon bishops in the seventh century. At its peak during the thirteenth century an estimated 3,000–5,000 people lived in Dunwich, making it one of England's largest settlements at that time. It was an international trading and fishing port and shipbuilding centre before a series of cataclysmic events eventually sealed the city's fate. Several storms and floods battered Dunwich in 1286 and 1287 and destroyed some of its buildings. Another severe storm in 1347 resulted in around 400 homes being lost to the sea. The port began silting up but for a while the citizens managed to keep it open. The so-called 'Grote Mandrenke' ('the drowning of men') in January 1362 was the final nail in the great city's coffin. More buildings disappeared beneath the waves and the course of the river was diverted to Walberswick. There was now no chance of Dunwich continuing to operate as a port and much of what was still standing was left to the mercy of the elements.

St Leonard's Church was claimed by the sea in the fourteenth century and St Martin's Church had completely vanished by the first decade of the fifteenth century. The Church of St Nicholas, said to be the old city's richest, went over the cliff edge during the late fifteenth century. St Peter's Church met the same fate around 200 years later. Two chapels, dedicated to St Francis and St Katherine respectively, succumbed to the sea in the late sixteenth century. A Knights Templar church founded in the late twelfth century was demolished during the 1560s and no trace remains. The same is true of the Blackfriars Dominion Priory, parts of which survived until the early eighteenth century. The last of the old city's churches to bite the proverbial dust was All Saints', which fell into the sea

The North Sea holds many secrets of ancient Dunwich.

in stages between 1904 and 1922. In the early 1990s the gravestone of John Brinkley Easey, who was buried in All Saints' churchyard in 1826, went over the cliff edge leaving just the gravestone of Jacob Forster, who passed away aged thirty-eight on 12 March 1796.

The ruins of Greyfriars Priory thankfully still exist, due partly to the fact that it was originally well inland. Now much closer to the cliff edge but not yet in danger of toppling over, the priory housed monks of the Franciscan order from the late thirteenth century until the Dissolution in 1538. The ruins are now in the care of Dunwich Greyfriars Trust. The remains of Dunwich Leper Chapel can still be seen in the churchyard of the present St James' Church completed in 1832. The chapel was part of a hospital for lepers built outside the old city during the twelfth century. The last remaining buttress of All Saints' Church was saved from the waves and rebuilt in St James' churchyard in 1923.

Parts of the submerged city have been located around 33 feet (10 metres) down by divers using sonar equipment in the inky blackness. Said to be the largest such site in Europe, inevitably it has become known as Britain's Atlantis. A fascinating model of the old city, showing just how much has been lost, is housed in Dunwich Museum. The present village has a population of fewer than 200 but throngs

Above and below: Greyfriars Priory ruins, Dunwich.

Above left: The last clifftop gravestone; *Above right*: All Saints' Church buttress, St James' churchyard, Dunwich.

with visitors during summer months. In the winter, when the tourists have gone, it seems to take on a more melancholic character. It is claimed that phantom figures and lights have been seen among the ruins of Greyfriars Priory. The chanting of monks has also been reported and even Black Shuck, the demon dog of East Anglia, is said to make the occasional visit.

Suffolk's 'Nessie': The Kessingland Sea Serpent

Sir Henry Rider Haggard, author of *King Solomon's Mines* and *She*, was working on a new book at Ditchingham House near Bungay in 1912 when he received a letter from his youngest daughter, nineteen-year-old Lilias. She was staying with friends at Kessingland Grange, the family's summer home just south of Lowestoft, when they witnessed a strange sight in the sea in front of the house. Lilias described a huge creature travelling at great speed and believed it to be 'a sea serpent'. In her letter dated 20 July 1912 she continued as follows:

> ...we could make out it had a sort of head at one end and then a series of about 30 pointed blobs which dwindled in size as they neared the tail. As it went along it seemed to get more and more submerged and then vanished. You can't imagine the pace it was going. I suppose it was about 60 feet (18.3 metres) long.

A sea serpent (Olaus Magnus, 1555).

After reading his daughter's letter, an intrigued Sir Henry travelled to Kessingland without delay and questioned Lilias and her companions about their experience. The cook and the gardener were both familiar with old tales of a sea serpent, though they do not appear to have witnessed the sighting. Rider Haggard sent his daughter's letter to the *Eastern Daily Press* with a covering letter, in which he asked if anyone else had seen the creature or could shed any light on the matter. Both letters were published in the newspaper on 24 July 1912. Nobody came forward to corroborate Lilias's sighting, though two people wrote in to confirm the legend of the Kessingland Sea Serpent. Sir Henry speculated that the sighting may 'have been a school of porpoises travelling at a great rate', an explanation that some readers agreed with.

The first written record of an unidentified 'monster' sighting at Kessingland appears to have been in the December 1750 edition of *The Gentleman's Magazine*. They reported it as follows:

The creature was about five feet (1.52 metres) long from what could be viewed of it above the water, with a head like a dog and a beard like a lion. The skin was spotted like that of a leopard. It passed in a leisurely fashion, finally disappearing beneath the waves to the great amazement of all those watching from the shore...

Around a century later one or more vague sightings of a sea beast were claimed, but perhaps the best documented case occurred in August 1923, when the captain

Neptune wrestles a sea serpent, South Pier, Lowestoft.

and navigator of HM *Kellet*, a survey vessel, reported an unexplained encounter. Captain F. E. B. Haselfoot recorded the incident:

> The time was about 9am. It was a summer day and the weather was calm and clear... I then observed rising out of the water about 200 yards (183 metres) from the ship, a long, serpentine neck, projecting from six or seven feet (1.8-2.1 metres) above the water. I observed this neck rising out of the water twice, and it remained up, in each case, for four or five seconds. Viewing with the naked eye only, I could not make out precisely what the head was like.

Lt Commander R. M. Southern, the ship's navigator, also briefly saw the raised neck and thought that it extended 'around eight to ten feet (2.4–3 metres)' above the waves.

The last known reported sighting took place in July 1978, when an anonymous holidaymaker claimed to have seen a 'long-necked creature' while walking on Kessingland beach. The man told the *East Anglian Magazine* that the sighting only lasted for a few seconds and admitted that he was already aware of the legend.

Some of the descriptions of the beast are very similar to those of the fabled Loch Ness Monster, though the 1750 sighting seems to have little in common with later reports. This was only a year after the Orford Sea Dragon (*see* following story) was caught. A number of other theories put forward to help explain the mystery include seal sightings, tricks of the light, a sandbank temporarily appearing above the waves, or even the giant oarfish, which may grow to around 50 feet (15.2 metres) in length but does not have a long neck or travel at great speed.

The Wild Man and Sea Dragon of Orford

Another peculiar story recorded by abbot and chronicler Ralph of Coggeshall, who also gave us the Green Children and Malekin tales, was that of the Wild Man of Orford. The story goes that around 1167 a strange creature was captured in the nets of local fishermen off the Suffolk coast and taken to Orford Castle, which at that time was newly built and incomplete. The unusual catch was described as being completely naked and resembling a man in size and form but covered with thick hair all over his body. He had a very bushy beard, though the crown of his head was bald. Ralph of Coggeshall, who was writing over thirty years after the event, mysteriously described his hair as 'pine-like'. He had a liking for raw fish, which he ate after squeezing them dry. The Wild Man was said to be an excellent swimmer but seemed unable to speak and communicated only with grunts. He was taken to church but appeared to have no understanding of his surroundings or religious symbols. The guards tortured their captive and hung him up by his feet in the castle dungeon but were unable to get any information from him. After being held prisoner for up to six months he was released back into the sea.

The story was retold by Suffolk man William Kirby (1759–1850), who gave a later date of *c.* 1204. He said that nets were placed to stop the Wild Man from travelling far out to sea but he simply swam underneath them. Sometime later, however, he came ashore again and lived on land for a while before returning to the sea for good. Other versions of the tale describe him as a monster or a merman with the tail of a fish. According to twentieth-century author W. A. Dutt, a pet seal kept at Orford Castle may have inspired the legend.

Another strange creature was hauled from the sea at Orford in 1749. It was said to resemble an alligator or crocodile but had wings, two legs and cloven feet. The unlikely catch was netted by mackerel fisherman who claimed that it

The quayside at Orford.

attacked two of the crew, mortally wounding one and injuring the other. The man who died had several fingers bitten off while the one who survived suffered lasting damage to his arm and hand. The beast then flew for a distance of around 50 yards (45.7 metres) before being killed by other fishermen. It was described as a 'Sea Dragon' and the body was exhibited around Suffolk for many years. The dried corpse was said to be covered with scales and around 4 feet (1.2 metres) long with five rows of sharp teeth in each jaw.

The description of the creature is similar to that of the mythical sea wyvern, a marine-dwelling dragon with wings but only two legs. One possible explanation is that it was a malformed specimen of alligator or crocodile, though neither is known for its ability to fly. It may have been a species of flying fish, but its remains went missing some time ago so a positive identification seems very unlikely.

Suffolk Smuggling

Smuggling or 'free trading' was widespread on the east coast during the seventeenth and eighteenth centuries. Highly taxed commodities such as alcohol, tobacco, tea and lace were the smugglers' stock in trade. For some it provided a lucrative living but was a dangerous occupation and clashes between the lawbreakers and the authorities were commonplace. Large-scale smuggling by ruthless organised gangs brought a swift response and soldiers were often deployed.

The Hadleigh Gang, once one of Suffolk's biggest and most feared groups of smugglers, were based in the south of the county in the market town from which they took their name. They controlled much of the smuggling that took place on the Suffolk coast, particularly in the area around Leiston, Sizewell and Aldeburgh. The Hadleigh Gang numbered up to 100 individuals and provided formidable opposition for the authorities. One encounter in 1735 at the George Inn in Hadleigh, where the gang managed to retake contraband goods seized by

Aldeburgh beach and 'Scallop' sculpture by Maggi Hambling CBE.

customs officers and soldiers, resulted in the death of a dragoon and a number of injuries. Two gang members were later hanged for their part in the incident. John Harvey, the gang leader, continued to clash with the authorities and was imprisoned before eventually being transported.

The White Hart Inn at Blythburgh was a haunt of both smugglers and dragoons drafted in to help protect the coast. Tobias Gill, a soldier better known as 'Black Toby' (*see* chapter 'More Mysterious Murders'), spent his last night as a free man there before being executed for allegedly murdering a local girl in 1750. Lurid stories about the ghosts of Toby and his supposed victim may have been invented or embellished by smugglers to help deter sightseers. The same could be said for some of the tales of the legendary Black Shuck.

The Anchor Inn at Walberswick was also well known for its smuggling connections. Physical evidence of this was found after it was demolished during the 1920s, when workmen discovered a bricked-up doorway in the cellar and the remains of a tunnel. This appeared to lead to the waterside and was probably used to secretly move smuggled goods. The present Anchor Inn stands in almost the same place as its predecessor.

Coastal communities were very tight knit and many of the locals were in some way associated with smuggling. They often resented the intervention of revenue men and the military. It was once claimed that at Orford only the vicar had nothing to do with smuggling. Legend has it that the rector of Pakefield near Lowestoft was once buried up to his neck in sand by smugglers when he complained about their illegal activities. They apparently dug him out just as the incoming tide was about to submerge him! Some men of the cloth, however, may have been persuaded to turn a blind eye in return for a bottle or two of something good. The following lines are taken from *The Smuggler's Song* by Rudyard Kipling:

The White Hart
Inn, Blythburgh.

Five and twenty ponies
Trotting through the dark -
Brandy for the parson
'Baccy for the clerk;
Laces for a lady; letters for a spy;
Watch the wall, my darling,
While the gentlemen go by.

Southwold Tales

In addition to its 102-foot-tall (31-metre) white lighthouse, the popular resort of Southwold is famous for the 18-pounder cannons that stand on Gun Hill. They look out on an area of ocean where a fierce naval battle took place in 1672, though the present cannons did not arrive until 1746. There is a legend that they were captured at the Battle of Culloden on 16 April 1746, when Charles Edward Stuart (also known as 'Bonnie Prince Charlie') was defeated by an army led by William Augustas, Duke of Cumberland. The Duke is said to have presented the guns to Southwold, though there appears to be no evidence that he ever visited the town. The more logical explanation is that they were sent by the Royal Armouries to offer some protection against possible future invaders.

Although never used in anger at Southwold, the guns were fired on ceremonial occasions, the last being in 1842 on the birthday of the Prince of Wales. Cannon number one failed to fire and the soldier in charge of the weapon looked down the barrel to check for any obstruction. At that moment it exploded and the soldier's head was blown off. The unlucky man was thirty-year-old James Martin, who was married with three young children. His ghost is claimed to occasionally appear on Gun Hill, sometimes but not always in headless form. The guns were buried during the First World War after the town came under heavy attack from

The town of
Southwold.

The Southwold cannons.

the Germans, who appeared to think they were operational. They were put back in position when hostilities ceased but removed again during the Second World War. As a result, nobody now knows which gun is cannon number one.

Another Southwold phantom is reputed to haunt Sutherland House on the High Street. Built in 1445 it was once the home of wealthy merchant Thomas Cammel, and the future James II stayed there intermittently during the Dutch War of 1665–72 when he was Duke of York. On the night before the Battle of Sole Bay, Edward Montague, Earl of Sandwich, apparently had a romantic liaison there with a sixteen-year-old serving maid. On the morning of 28 May 1672, Montague was late to arrive at his ship to take part in the battle against a massive Dutch fleet estimated to number between seventy and ninety ships. They were carrying a total of over 20,000 men and more than 4,000 guns and were pitted against a combined fleet of British and French vessels. The result was inconclusive but both sides claimed victory. The British and the Dutch each lost two ships and around 1,800–2,000 men. Montague was killed during the battle and the grieving maid is said to have died from a broken heart soon after. Her presence has been felt on a number of occasions in a bedroom in Sutherland House, now a hotel and restaurant (*see* chapter 'Haunted Hostelries').

Montague House, Southwold.

Plaque on the front of Montague House.

One of Southwold's most famous former residents is Eric Blair, better known as author George Orwell. The Blair family moved to Southwold in 1921 and after serving with the Imperial Police in Burma and living in Paris and London, Orwell returned to Southwold in 1929 where he spent much of the next six years. His novel *A Clergyman's Daughter* (1935) was inspired by his friendship with Brenda Salkeld, herself the daughter of a clergyman and a gymnastics teacher at St Felix Girls' School in Southwold. She turned down his offer of marriage but the two remained friends. Orwell, who was suffering from tuberculosis, died on 21 January 1950 when an artery burst in his lungs. He was forty-six years old.

A new commemorative plaque was unveiled by Orwell's adopted son Richard Blair on 20 May 2018, on the front wall of Montague House on Southwold High Street, where he lived and wrote for several years. A large mural of Orwell was painted on the back of the Pier Café during the town's 2014 Arts Festival.

Walberswick Tales

The small coastal resort of Walberswick is very popular with modern tourists but also has more than its expected share of odd stories.

The aforementioned George Orwell had a brush with the supernatural in Walberswick and described his experience in a letter to a friend named

'Haunted' ruins, St Andrew's churchyard, Walberswick.

Dennis Collings. While sitting in the ruins of a late fifteenth-century church in St Andrew's churchyard, he saw a male figure pass through an archway. He followed but found no further trace of it. Orwell described the figure as being 'small and stooping and dressed in lightish brown' and concluded that it 'had therefore vanished, presumably a hallucination'. He drew a sketch showing where the sighting took place and gave the date and time as 27 July 1931 at around 5.20 p.m. After making enquiries he found that he was not the first to report an encounter with the unknown apparition. Other eyewitnesses have described the figure, which has also been seen elsewhere in the general locality, as resembling 'a Victorian gentleman' or 'a churchwarden'.

Walberswick Ferry, which takes travellers over the river to Southwold, has long been the subject of strange tales. Several people have reported seeing an old man holding a small child by the hand, apparently waiting to board the ferry. The ferryman, however, appears to ignore or not see them and sets off leaving the pair still standing on the riverbank. During the early twentieth century when the ferryman was known as Old Todd, a visitor pointed out to him that two passengers had failed to board the ferry. The ferryman's terse reply was, 'We never wait for *them*!' The visitor turned round but the phantoms had disappeared. Old Todd would not elaborate but the visitor later discovered that his was not the first such sighting. Since then the ghostly duo have been seen intermittently but I am unaware of any recent reports. Some have speculated that they may have once been real flesh and blood passengers who drowned when the ferry sank or capsized, though it is uncertain whether such a tragedy actually happened.

A presence of a very different kind apparently frequents Walberswick Common. A large white pointer-like dog has been reported on a number of occasions over the last century or more. It is said to hide in the bracken until someone approaches, when it suddenly rises and silently trots away. The most high-profile sighting was by author Penelope Fitzgerald, who claimed that a pony she was taking across the common refused to move any further when they chanced upon the mysterious dog. After it loped away making no sound the pony was happy to walk on. Though quite well known in the area, there is no clue as to

Walberswick Ferry.

the creature's identity or why it continues to haunt the common. This particular entity does not appear to travel further afield and seems to have no connection with other phantom dog stories.

Another strange local tale of the Walberswick Whisperers or Whistlers was recorded by Peter Haining in his book *The Supernatural Coast*. The late author claimed that for many years people in the area – particularly women – had heard unexplained noises that some considered to be of supernatural origin. Mr Haining suggested that the phenomenon may have been an inspiration for M. R. James' popular ghost story *Oh, Whistle and I'll come to You, My Lad* (1904).

A Peter Pan Village and the House in the Clouds

On approaching Thorpeness along the narrow coast road from Aldeburgh, a mysterious edifice can be seen from a distance. Incredibly, it appears to be a country cottage suspended high above the treetops. This is no optical illusion but the famous House in the Clouds, the centrepiece of a fantasy village. The coastal holiday location of Thorpeness as it appears today is the relatively recent realisation of one man's slightly whimsical dream and has been called 'the weirdest village in Britain'. Glencairn Stuart Ogilvie, a Scottish barrister, architect and playwright, was fifty years old when in 1908 he inherited the 6,000-acre estate from his father, Alexander Ogilvie, who had become very wealthy as an internationally successful railway engineer. Thorpe was originally a fishing hamlet rumoured to be popular with smugglers, but Ogilvie added 'ness' to its name and transformed the remote location into a magical village of grandiose and unique buildings, a large boating lake, a golf course, tennis courts and even a railway station.

The House in the Clouds, Thorpeness.

It is said that after part of the estate was flooded in 1910, Ogilvie remarked, 'Let's keep it and build a holiday village around it.' A lake, just 2 feet 6 inches (.76 metres) deep, was dug and named the Meare. Several channels and miniature islands were also constructed and given a Peter Pan theme. Wendy's House, Crocodile's Lake and Pirate's Lair were all inspired by the book written by J. M. Barrie, a friend of the Ogilvie family. The village itself was constructed during the 1910s and '20s and the cleverly disguised five-storey water tower with a 'cottage' on top was erected in 1923. It stands 70 feet (21.3 metres) tall and the staircase to the top has sixty-eight steps. A 50,000-gallon water tank (later reduced to 30,000 gallons after being hit by 'friendly' fire during the Second World War) was installed on the top floor with residential accommodation beneath. The building was named the House in the Clouds by Mrs Malcolm Mason, a children's author who bravely lived in the tower beneath the enormous water tank. A poem written by her in 1923 includes the following lines:

> The fairies really own this house
> Or so the children say,
> In fact, they all of them moved in
> Upon the self same day.

A post windmill originally built in 1803 at nearby Aldringham was moved to Thorpeness in 1922/23 and converted to pump water to its new neighbour. The water tank was taken out in 1979 and a games room now occupies the space under the pitched roof. The House in the Clouds is available to let as a holiday retreat and the windmill was restored to working order by 2015. Both buildings are situated alongside a track from the main road through the village. Thorpeness is a magnet for tourists during summer months and has many unique charms and eccentricities.

Thorpeness Meare.

Legends of Edmund: King, Martyr and Saint

Many tales have been told of King Edmund, also known as St Edmund and Edmund the Martyr. He is said to have been born in AD 841 and to have been crowned King of the East Angles at Bures in Suffolk on Christmas Day, 855 (or 856), aged just fourteen or fifteen. These dates, like almost all the information about him, cannot be verified as the earliest surviving record of his existence was written after his death. Abbo, a monk and abbot of Fleury Abbey near Orleans in France, wrote about Edmund in or around 986, though several of the more elaborate stories come from the pen of Roger of Wendover, a thirteenth-century chronicler noted for his entertaining and flamboyant style of writing.

According to legend, when East Anglia was under attack from the Vikings a great battle took place near Thetford between the invaders and the East Angles led by Edmund. Many were killed on both sides but the king survived and made a camp with his depleted army at Hoxne in Suffolk. Aware that his enemies were closing in, Edmund hid beneath Goldbrook Bridge but was betrayed by a wedding party passing overhead. They saw his golden spurs shining in the sun and told the Danes where he could be found. After being captured he was offered a stark choice: renounce his Christianity to save his life or endure a painful death. Edmund chose the latter. He was tied to a tree in a nearby wood, tortured

Goldbrook
Bridge, Hoxne.

The betrayal of Edmund, St Edmund's Hall, Hoxne.

and 'shot through with arrows', then his head was cut off and tossed into the undergrowth. This is said to have taken place on 20 November 869 or 870.

Edmund's followers quickly recovered his severely punctured body but could not find his head. Sometime later they searched the wood, calling out 'where are you?', and a cry came back, 'here, here, here!' To their astonishment they found an old grey wolf with Edmund's severed head between its paws. The wolf, which seemed to be guarding the head, let his followers take it but stayed close by until the king's remains were buried. A simple wooden chapel was erected over Edmund's grave. William of Malmesbury, a respected twelfth-century historian and chronicler, told the tale of a blind man and a boy who took overnight shelter in the chapel. A fierce storm was raging outside but, as dawn broke, the weather was transformed and the man's sight was restored. This was the first of many miracles attributed to Edmund which led to him being declared a saint. After being exhumed and removed to Beodericsworth – later renamed Bury St Edmunds in his honour – around thirty years later, Edmund's head and body were found to have fused together and the only clue that they had once been separated was a thin red line around the neck. Furthermore, the numerous arrow holes had healed and the body was still fresh. Edmund was reinterred in a church which was later rebuilt by King Cnut (Canute). A thriving abbey was established and a grand shrine was constructed to house Edmund's remains. His coffin was reopened several times and his hair and nails were alleged to still be growing.

Memorial stone, Goldbrook Bridge

Edmund's monument, Hoxne.

A woman named Oswen cut them annually and in 1198, over 300 years after his death, the head and body were confirmed to still be connected with no sign of decomposition. A mute woman named Aelfgern, who walked alone from Winchester to Edmund's shrine, gradually found the ability to converse and this was hailed as yet another miracle.

Edmund's shrine was destroyed in 1539 but there is a legend that his remains were stolen in 1217 and taken to Toulouse in France. Some relics claimed to be his were given to Arundel Castle in West Sussex in 1901 and there they remain, though their authenticity is disputed and some bones appear to belong to a female. Some believe that the former King of East Anglia's body was never taken at all and that he still lies among the ruins of Bury Abbey. An article in *The Telegraph* in May 2017 suggested that he could lie beneath tennis courts in Abbey Gardens, echoing the discovery of Richard III's remains under a car park in Leicester in 2012. The tennis courts are believed to be on the site of a monks' cemetery.

Statues of Edmund: St Edmund's Hall, Hoxne (*below left*) and St Edmund's Church, Southwold (*below right*).

Edmund allegedly put a curse on Goldbrook Bridge in Hoxne when the wedding party betrayed him and the present bridge, which dates from 1878, is a place that modern couples still avoid on their way to tie the knot. St Edmund's Hall, which stands beside the bridge and now serves as Hoxne village hall, was built by Sir Edward Kerrison in 1879 and features a depiction of the king being betrayed and a rooftop statue of him. A monument in a nearby field marks the spot where he was supposedly executed. The tree to which he was tied – known as St Edmund's Oak – split apart in 1843 and an arrowhead was reportedly found inside it. Alternatively, it may have been a twisted piece of wire! Other statues of Edmund can be found in Bury St Edmunds and over the front porch of St Edmund's Church, Southwold.

  Various conflicting theories give Edmund's place of execution and original burial as either Bradfield St Clare, south of Bury St Edmunds; Hellesdon near Norwich in Norfolk; Lyng in Norfolk; Dernford in Cambridgeshire; or Maldon in Essex. Abbo gave the location as Haegelisdun, which has long been associated with Hoxne, but this is contested by a number of historians and authors. St Edmund was the original patron saint of England before being usurped by St George the dragon slayer. In the present century there have already been two unsuccessful campaigns to have Edmund reinstated as England's patron saint.

Anne Boleyn's Heart and Other Stories

The Legend of Queen Anne Boleyn's Heart

Nobody knows for certain exactly when or where Anne Boleyn was born. Her year of birth was probably sometime between 1501 and 1507, while Blickling Hall in Norfolk and Hever Castle in Kent both lay claims to being her birthplace. She is believed to have lived for part of her life at the original Blickling Hall on the site of the present Jacobean mansion, but also had strong connections with Suffolk.

It is common knowledge that King Henry VIII's second wife parted company with her head during a violent execution on 19 May 1536, after being found guilty of adultery on dubious evidence. Less well known is a tale that her heart was also removed and buried in St Mary's Church, Erwarton, in south-east Suffolk. Anne resided for at least a short while with her aunt Amata at Erwarton Hall, and her future husband is believed to have visited her there. She loved the area so much that she wanted her heart to be buried at St Mary's Church, and an uncle is said to have ensured that her wish was respected. A lead casket in the shape of a heart was discovered during work at the church around 1838 and

Queen Anne Boleyn. (Hans Holbein; courtesy of the Wellcome Collection CC BY-4.0)

Erwarton Church. (Photo © Keith Evans - geograph.org.uk - CC-BY-SA/2.0)

reburied under the organ. The casket was opened and apparently contained dust but there appears to have been no inscription to definitely link it with the former queen. According to a plaque marking the place where the casket was reburied, the uncle was Sir Phillip Parker but it now seems more likely that it was Sir Phillip Calthorpe, who married Anne's aunt Amata.

It is generally accepted that Anne Boleyn's body – either with or without her heart and possibly minus her head – was buried in the chapel of St Peter ad Vincula at the Tower of London, and an elm chest thought to contain her remains was discovered there during renovations in the 1870s. Nevertheless, another legend claims that after her beheading Anne's body was secretly taken to Salle Church in Norfolk, where some of her ancestors were interred. There it was buried under an anonymous black slab following a nocturnal funeral service. In addition to Salle Church and Blickling Hall, Anne's restless ghost allegedly haunts the Tower of London, Hever Castle, Hampton Court Palace, Marwell Hall and Caister Castle.

Simon of Sudbury's Severed Head

Like Anne Boleyn, former Archbishop of Canterbury Simon of Sudbury also parted company with his head at the Tower of London, though in quite different circumstances. He was born in Sudbury around 1316–18 and was appointed Bishop of London in 1361 before becoming Archbishop of Canterbury in 1375. During the Peasants' Revolt of 1381, he was inside the Tower and seemingly safe from the baying mob outside who were angry that in his other role as Chancellor he had introduced a much-hated early form of poll tax. Led by Wat Tyler, the rebels demanded a meeting with fourteen-year-old King Richard II at Mile End, during which the beleaguered monarch conceded to several of their demands. This was obviously not enough to pacify the rebels as they then marched to the Tower determined to take revenge on the man they held most responsible for their plight. Once there, it appears that they were allowed access to the normally heavily guarded fortress and took the Archbishop prisoner. They then dragged him outside and finally managed to remove his head, though this apparently required eight blows of an axe! The Treasurer, Sir Robert Hales, who had been praying with Simon in St John's Chapel, was also beheaded. The Archbishop's severed head was then carried around the streets before being impaled on a pole over the gatehouse of London Bridge. Wat Tyler's head replaced Simon's on the pole a few days later, when he was executed for attempting to stab the Mayor of London and a royal valet.

Simon's head was returned to his home town and placed inside St Gregory's Church, where it remains to this day. It was once on public display but is now kept in a locked compartment in the vestry wall. If having his head chopped off was not enough, poor Simon suffered the further indignity of having his teeth removed and sold off to relic hunters. Inevitably, it is claimed that his ghost has been seen inside St Gregory's and that phantom footsteps have been heard.

St Gregory's Church, Sudbury. (Photo © Adrian Cable - geograph.org.uk - CC-BY-SA/2.0)

Perhaps he is looking for his head, or for his decapitated body which was buried at Canterbury Cathedral. It seems strange that his head and body have never been reunited – and even odder that a cannonball was reputedly buried in his grave in place of his missing head!

In the present century, Simon of Sudbury's skull was analysed by a forensic artist and an accurate recreation of his head and face was unveiled in St Gregory's Church on 15 September 2011.

The Last Maharajah

Suffolk and Norfolk both claim strong connections with Duleep Singh, the last Maharajah of the Punjab. He was born on 4 September 1838 in Lahore, at that time the capital of the Sikh Empire. The son of Maharajah Ranjit Singh, nicknamed the 'Lion of the Punjab', he became ruler of the Sikh Empire at the age of five following the assassinations of the four previous maharajahs. His mother, Maharani Jind Kaur, acted as Regent. After the two Anglo-Sikh Wars, Duleep Singh was deposed from power in 1849 and held under guard in India before being exiled to Britain in 1854. Following a sojourn at Claridge's Hotel in London, he briefly lived in Wimbledon and Roehampton, and was also a guest of Queen Victoria and Prince Albert at Osborne House on the Isle of Wight. The Queen in particular was said to be captivated by the young maharajah. After returning from a tour of Europe in 1855, Duleep Singh relocated to Perthshire, Scotland. His mother, who had earlier been held prisoner in India, was finally allowed to join her son in Britain in 1861, two years before her death.

Maharajah Duleep Singh's grave, Elveden churchyard.

In 1863 Duleep Singh moved into a 17,000-acre estate at Elveden, Suffolk, which began his family's long association with the region. He made many improvements to Elveden Hall and turned the estate into a game park. In 1886 he was detained in Aiden while attempting to return to India. After reconverting to Sikhism, having been 'persuaded' to become a Christian at the age of fourteen, he was forced to return to Europe and passed away aged fifty-five in Paris on 22 October 1893. Against his wishes, Maharajah Duleep Singh was laid to rest in Elveden churchyard instead of his body being returned to India for cremation. His grave is next to those of his first wife, Maharani Bamba Duleep Singh, who died aged thirty-nine on 18 September 1887, and youngest son, Albert Edward Alexander Duleep Singh, who passed away at the age of thirteen on 1 May 1893.

The last maharajah is still fondly remembered on both sides of the Norfolk/Suffolk border and a plaque given by the Sikhs of the United Kingdom was unveiled in Elveden churchyard on the centenary of his death. A grand life-sized bronze statue of him astride a horse was installed at Butten Island, Thetford, in 1999. It was officially unveiled by HRH the Prince of Wales. Duleep Singh married twice and had a total of eight children. One of his sons, Prince Frederick Victor Duleep Singh (1868–1926), served as an officer in both the Suffolk and Norfolk Yeomanry and during the First World War was stationed in France for two years. Prince Frederick presented the Ancient House to the town of Thetford for use as

Maharajah Duleep Singh's statue, Thetford.

a museum. One of the maharajah's daughters, Princess Sophia Alexandra Duleep Singh (1876–1948), became a leading suffragette and was commemorated on a stamp issued by the Royal Mail in February 2018.

Tall Tales: The Newbourne Giants

Two Suffolk brothers with a combined height of nearly 15 feet (4.57 metres) were born during the nineteenth century in the small village of Newbourne, situated to the east of Ipswich. George Page was said to be 7 feet 7 inches (2.32 metres) tall and his brother Meadows 7 feet 4 inches (2.23 metres). No other family member was tall and their father, George 'Pippin' Page, was just 5 feet 5 inches (1.65 metres) in height. The oversized brothers were both employed as farm labourers and lived with their parents and four sisters in a small cottage which originally had just two bedrooms. Neither George jnr nor Meadows could stand upright inside their home as the ceilings were only 6 feet 5 inches (1.96 metres) high.

The family was poor and found it difficult to make ends meet. For a while it looked like the brothers' stature could be a passport to a brighter future, but this was not to be. They both joined Samuel Whiting's travelling show in 1869 after making an appearance at an Easter fair in Woodbridge. They were exhibited far and wide as the Newbourne Giants and George was also billed separately as the Suffolk Giant. As with many such shows around this time, scant regard was paid to the well-being of the 'exhibits'. Living conditions were squalid and both brothers were badly treated. George, who had been suffering from a severe chest infection, died almost exactly a year after joining the show. He was just twenty-six years old. His headstone in the churchyard of St Mary's Church in Newbourne is now difficult to read but carries the following inscription:

> Sacred to the memory of George Page, the Suffolk Giant, who died April 28th, 1870, in his 26th year. He was exhibited in most towns in England but his best exhibition was with his Blessed Redeemer.

After the death of his taller sibling, Meadows Page continued to tour for another five years before a knife was ominously left in his caravan. Now the father of a baby girl, he took the unsubtle hint and wisely decided to leave the travelling life behind. Meadows returned to his former occupation of farm labourer and lived for a further forty-two years. Upon his death in 1917 he too was buried in the churchyard at Newbourne. Felixstowe-based author John Owen was inspired to write his novel *The Giant of Oldbourne* in 1926 after visiting the churchyard.

George Page seems to have been of similar height to Robert Hales, the Norfolk Giant. Hales, who died aged fifty in 1863, became a rich man after touring America with P. T. Barnum's circus and twice met Queen Victoria. Perhaps if George Page had lived longer he would be better known today. Nevertheless, the

Newbourne Church. (Photo © Adrian Cable - geograph.org.uk - CC-BY-SA/2.0)

Page brothers are fondly remembered in and around the Newbourne area. The house where the family lived still exists and has been enlarged. It was advertised for sale at £615,000 in May 2018.

The Poacher's Story

An autobiography by an anonymous author was first published in 1935 under the pseudonym 'The King of the Norfolk Poachers'. *I Walked by Night* told the story of someone who lived much of his life on the wrong side of the law and served several prison sentences. The poacher's exploits in the dead of night and the often cruel methods he used to trap animals made up much of the story, which was illustrated by local artist Edward Seago.

The identity of the mystery author has since been revealed as Frederick Rolfe, who was born in Pentney, Norfolk, in 1862, but spent the last two decades of his life in Suffolk, where he is buried. Rolfe, a former gamekeeper, enjoyed pitting his wits against the authorities and only poor health in his later years prevented him from continuing his nocturnal activities. He put down his life story in an exercise book which he gave to Mrs Longrigg, the wife of a local farmer who had employed him as a mole catcher. Sometime later, she passed it to a neighbour, author Lilias Rider Haggard, the youngest daughter of celebrated novelist Sir Henry Rider Haggard. She edited Rolfe's manuscript and in the book's introduction wrote the following:

What is written here was born of an old man's loneliness, as he sat in a little cottage perched high on a hill, overlooking the Waveney Valley, with no company but his dog. The life that he loved had passed him by...

Frederick Rolfe lived for the last fourteen years of his life at No. 15 Nethergate Street, Bungay, as the lodger of Mrs Jessie Redgrave. At 3.35 p.m. on 23 March 1938, Rolfe's body was found by a policeman, hanging from a wire snare attached to a beam in a shed at No. 1 Nethergate Street. His landlady had reported him missing after she found a note from him that morning. The coroner's verdict was that 'death was due to asphyxiation by hanging, self-inflicted, whilst the balance of his mind was disturbed'. Frederick Rolfe lies in an unmarked grave in Bungay cemetery.

Various artefacts including his guns, photographs, and the handwritten manuscript of *I Walked by Night* are preserved in Bungay Museum. Though parts of Rolfe's book may be inaccurate and misleading, particularly the sections relating to his two marriages and his children, it still provides a fascinating glimpse into a shadowy side of East Anglian history.

Nethergate Street, Bungay.

Maria Marten and the Red Barn Murder

The murder of Maria Marten in Polstead, 5 miles south-west of Hadleigh, was one of the most talked about killings of the nineteenth century. It remains one of the best-known British murders and probably the most famous – or infamous – ever committed in Suffolk. Whole books have been written about the Red Barn Murder, as it is often known, along with several plays, films, and the BBC Television drama *Maria Marten* (1980).

Maria Marten was born on 24 July 1801 and went missing from her home on Friday 18 May 1827. She was never seen alive again and her partly decomposed body was finally found by her father buried inside the Red Barn in Polstead on 19 April 1828. He began digging there after his much younger second wife Ann supposedly had vivid dreams that mysteriously revealed the whereabouts of Maria's corpse. Ann Marten was only a year older than her stepdaughter and her evidence would play a decisive part in the trial and conviction of Maria's killer.

During her short but eventful life the unmarried Maria Marten had three children by three different fathers, which at that time was considered scandalous. The father of her third child was William Corder, a young farmer and landowner born in 1803. Their son was born in 1827 but died within a few weeks, as

Maria Marten's cottage, Polstead, 1828. (Courtesy of the Wellcome Collection CC PDM 1.0)

had another of Maria's children fathered by Corder's older brother Thomas. According to her stepmother, Maria was planning to elope with William Corder. Ann Marten would later testify that Corder called at the family home on 18 May and told Maria to meet him at the Red Barn. Soon after he left the cottage, Maria followed to keep the fateful rendezvous with her lover. Nothing more was heard from Maria but Corder wrote letters to her family stating that he and his new wife had moved to the Isle of Wight. The uncertainty continued for almost a year before Ann Marten's dreams guided her husband Thomas to the gruesome discovery of Maria's body.

William Corder naturally became the police's number one suspect and he was quickly found in Brentford running a ladies' boarding house with Mary Moore, whom he had married after leaving Suffolk. She was reportedly one of over 100 women who had replied to advertisements placed by Corder in several national newspapers, and had no knowledge of his chequered past. At his trial in August 1828, Corder denied murder and claimed that his lover had shot herself after they had an argument in the Red Barn. It was thought that Maria probably died from a gunshot wound, though she may also have been stabbed in the eye with a short sword. Corder's handkerchief was found tied around her neck and an iron spike had been driven through her hip. Spikes were sometimes used to try to prevent the spirit of a person from wandering, particularly those thought to be vampires or witches.

Ann Marten's evidence, particularly the revelation that Maria came to her in dreams to reveal her sordid fate, was lapped up by the public and the press. The jury took just over half an hour to find Corder guilty of Maria Marten's murder. He was

The Red Barn, Polstead, 1828. (Courtesy of the Wellcome Collection CC PDM 1.0)

publically hanged on 11 August 1828 in Bury St Edmunds and reportedly confessed to the murder while on the gallows. A crowd of up to 20,000 people attended his execution. Corder's body was slit open and put on public display at the Shire Hall later that day. It was then dissected in front of medical students and his skeleton was used in anatomy classes at the West Suffolk Hospital until the 1940s. A book of the trial bound with Corder's skin can be seen in Moyse's Hall Museum in Bury St Edmunds, along with his scalp and hair, his pistols and a replica death mask. Norwich Castle Museum has another replica death mask in its dungeon.

The execution of William Corder, 1828. (Courtesy of the Wellcome Collection CC BY-4.0)

In the aftermath of Corder's trial and execution, a huge number of sightseers descended on the remote village of Polstead. It was estimated that during 1828 alone it was besieged by around 200,000 visitors. Many removed and took home pieces of the Red Barn as souvenirs and only the shell was still standing when it was mysteriously destroyed by fire in 1842. The barn was considered a place of ill omen long before the murder took place and acquired its name due to the setting sun bathing it in a blood-red glow. Maria Marten was buried on 20 April 1828 in St Mary's churchyard, but even her gravestone was not immune to the fanatical attentions of souvenir hunters. Piece by piece it was chipped away until nothing was left by the turn of the century. It was not replaced but a simple wooden tablet was placed on a shed a short distance from her grave. It hardly seems a fitting memorial but anything grander may well fall prey to modern 'collectors'. The church itself is very much as it was in Maria's time.

There has been much speculation as to whether Maria's stepmother knew from the start where she was buried and simply invented the 'dreams' story. Some authors have suggested that Ann Marten may also have been having an affair with Corder, and exacted revenge on him when he failed to return to collect her after killing Maria. Samuel 'Beauty' Smith, a shadowy figure and career criminal who had numerous convictions for theft, has also been linked with the murder. He and Corder were well known to each other and Smith was rumoured to have been in Polstead at the time of the killing. Some have claimed that he assisted

Polstead Church.

Maria Marten's
plaque, Polstead
Church.

Corder in the crime or even fired the fatal shot. However, none of the various
theories are supported by hard evidence. Mystery also surrounds the burial place
of Corder and Marten's young son. The pair both said that he was buried in
Sudbury, yet no record of such a burial has ever been found. It is assumed that he
was buried in unconsecrated ground, which has inevitably raised the question of
whether his death was suspicious.

The pretty village of Polstead still feels very isolated today and retains much
of its rural charm. The family's cottage still exists on Marten's Lane and the site
of the Red Barn – now just an open field – is further along the same narrow road
roughly opposite the entrance to Frog's Hall. Corder's House still stands in the
centre of the village opposite a large pond and not far from the church. Like the
Marten's cottage it is a Grade II listed building. Both properties are privately
owned and are not open to the public.

More Mysterious Murders

In addition to the Red Barn Murder, Suffolk, like virtually every other county, has seen its share of bloody killings over the centuries. The disturbing cases described below are very different but all have intriguing, mysterious and sometimes paranormal tales attached to them.

Unsolved Murder in Peasenhall

William Harsent was greeted by a terrible sight when he called at the back entrance of Providence House in Peasenhall, near Saxmundham, at 8 a.m. on Sunday 1 June 1902. He was delivering newly laundered clothes for his daughter Rose, who worked as a live-in maid servant at the property. He found the door open and walked in to find his daughter's lifeless body covered in blood from stab wounds to her throat, shoulders and chest. Rose was wearing just socks and a nightdress which had been set alight. A broken oil lamp, a smashed medicine bottle and burned newspaper fragments were scattered around her body.

The former Providence House, Peasenhall.

The police originally suspected that Miss Harsent had committed suicide, but soon realised that she had been murdered. In fact, it was a double killing as the victim was found to be six months pregnant. This came as a surprise to her parents and her elderly employers, Mr and Mrs Crisp. The main suspect was William Gardiner, a thirty-five-year-old married man and father of six who lived and worked in Peasenhall and was also a senior member of the local Primitive Methodist Church. Rose Harsent sang in the church choir and it was rumoured that she and Gardiner may have been having an affair. This was mainly due to claims by two local youths, George Wright and Alfonso Skinner, that they saw the pair enter a small building used as a chapel on 1 May 1901 and heard 'intimate' sounds from within. The youths made sure that Gardiner's alleged indiscretions with an 'innocent' young woman soon became the talk of the village. He strongly denied the accusations and threatened them both with legal action if they persisted. Wright and Skinner would later retell somewhat embellished accounts of the incident in court.

The police found a number of letters in the deceased's bedroom including an anonymous one which read as follows:

Peasenhall village.

Dear R., I will try to see you tonight at 12 o'clock at your place if you put a light in your window at 10 o'clock for about ten minutes, then you can take it out again. Don't have a light in your room at 12 as I will come round to the back.

Two letters written by William Gardiner to Rose Harsent soon after the alleged incident in the chapel, in which he expressed regret that their good names had been besmirched by unfounded allegations, were also found. One handwriting expert was of the opinion that the anonymous letter had been written by the same hand, though others were unsure. The broken medicine bottle found at the murder scene contained paraffin and was labelled, 'For Mrs Gardiner's children'. Georgina Gardiner, wife of the accused, testified that she gave Rose the bottle filled with camphorated oil because she had a cold. The newspaper used to start the fire which burned the victim's nightdress and lower body was one that William Gardiner was known to regularly read. However, the Gardiners' neighbour, Mrs Dickinson, claimed that they were both at her house during a thunderstorm from around 11.30 p.m. on Saturday 31 May until at least 1.30 the following morning. Another neighbour, Henry Burgess, said that he and William Gardiner had a conversation about the weather at around 10 p.m. on 31 May.

Rose Harsent's grave,
Peasenhall cemetery.

William Gardiner pleaded 'not guilty' when the first murder trial began in Ipswich on 7 November 1902, but the jury was unable to reach a unanimous verdict. All jury members except one believed that Gardiner was guilty, but at the retrial in January 1903, all but one felt that he was either innocent or his guilt had not been proved. The prosecutor was Henry Fielding Dickens, son of author Charles Dickens. The option of a third trial was considered but rejected and Gardiner walked free, though he was never officially declared innocent. The Gardiner family quickly left Peasenhall for a new life in the London area. William Gardiner died in 1941 aged seventy-four.

Rose Annie Harsent may have been born in March 1879. She was laid to rest in Peasenhall cemetery on 5 June 1902. Providence House still exists as a private residence close to St Michael's Church but has been renamed. Almost as well known as the Polstead Red Barn Murder, the case is still the subject of much speculation. Some believe that a jealous Georgina Gardiner may have carried out the murder, but she had the same alibi as her prime suspect husband. In court the defence pointed the finger at twenty-year-old Frederick Davis, who lived next door to Miss Harsent. He admitted that he wrote 'pornographic' poetry for Rose and supplied her with a book on pregnancy termination, but denied that he was her killer or the father of her unborn child. He was never charged and the judge dismissed the defence's claims. Well over a century later the mystery remains unsolved.

Tobias Gill: Guilty or Innocent?

The body of a Walberswick girl named Ann (or Anne) Blakemore was discovered one morning in late June 1750, on common land at Blythburgh. Close by was a black soldier named Tobias Gill, a drummer with the 4th Dragoons under the command of Sir Robert Rich. Gill had been drinking heavily at the nearby White Hart public house the night before and was still sleeping off his excesses. He denied any knowledge of the girl's death but was charged with her murder and imprisoned in Ipswich while awaiting trial. Known by the nickname 'Black Toby', he was found guilty at Bury Assizes on 25 August 1750 and sentenced to death. He protested his innocence to the last and unsuccessfully requested to be tied to the back of a moving mail coach as an alternative to hanging. Instead he was hanged on 14 September at the spot where Ann Blakemore's body was found. Toby's corpse was dipped in tar and hung in chains from a gibbet, and there it remained for several months. The gibbet eventually collapsed around half a century later.

Though some accounts state that Miss Blakemore was brutally raped in addition to being murdered, the coroner declared that her body showed no visible signs of injury and her clothing had not been disturbed. There are also inconsistencies regarding Gill's exact whereabouts when the girl's body was found. Some versions of the story have him lying directly beside her, while others suggest that he may not have been present at the scene but became the

Toby's Walks, Blythburgh.

prime suspect mainly due to his reputation as a drunkard. Modern authors have speculated that racial prejudice may have played a part in his conviction and that the girl possibly died from natural causes. The Dragoons were unpopular in the locality as they were sent to combat widespread smuggling, an illicit trade that many citizens were in some way involved with.

The exact location of the alleged murder and subsequent execution is disputed but it may have been in or close to a rather bleak area now known as Toby's Walks. Tobias Gill's ghost is reputed to haunt the locality, either on foot or driving a phantom black coach drawn by four headless horses. Toby himself is sometimes said to be headless. A building known as Toby's Barn was believed to be haunted but no trace of it remains. An apparition in a blue dress, assumed to be Ann Blakemore, is said to run out in front of oncoming traffic in late June. Whether Tobias Gill really was a drunken murderer or an innocent scapegoat will never be known. In any event, it is probably advisable to avoid the area after dark!

The Letheringham Watermill Murders

Two gruesome murders took place at the isolated Letheringham Watermill in rural Suffolk in the late 1690s. Located to the north of Wickham Market, the watermill was run by miller John Bullard and his son, also named John. They

Potsford Wood Gallows. (Photo © Keith Evans - geograph.org.uk - CC-BY-SA/2.0)

employed a man called Jonah Snell, which in light of what happened next turned out to be a bad decision.

As they were doing their accounts one day, Snell viciously attacked his employers with an axe and left them both in a pool of blood. He then hung them upside down from a beam inside the mill. When the butchered bodies were discovered, Snell still had the bloodstained axe in his possession and was said to be wandering around as if dazed. He was found guilty of the double murder and sentenced to death at his trial in Wickham Market. Little is known about Snell and his motive for the murders. Whether they were premeditated or spur of the moment is impossible to say, for he offered no explanation or defence for his crimes.

Jonah Snell was hanged in chains at Potsford Wood near Wickham Market on 14 April 1699. His body was left to decay in an iron-cage gibbet until only the skeleton remained as a warning to other would-be axe-murderers. Eventually Snell's sorry bones were buried in an unmarked grave in the wood and the story was largely forgotten as the centuries rolled by. During the late 1950s the remains of the gibbet post were found by workers clearing undergrowth in the wood. Research revealed the horrific murders and the historic significance of the gibbet. It was decided that the post should be put back in position and that railings should be erected around it. A plaque bearing the words 'Last known hanging 14 April 1699 (Jonah Snell)' was attached to the post.

This macabre memorial is claimed to be the focus for paranormal activity. An unnamed lorry driver, who stopped at Potsford Wood in the 1980s to answer a call of nature, swore that he encountered a hooded skeletal figure there after an icy hand tapped him on the shoulder. In 1997, a couple whose car broke down nearby reported seeing a 'black shapeless apparition' in the wood. Others have allegedly heard the rattling of chains and seen strange lights. Paranormal investigators claim to have picked up unexplained noises on their recording equipment.

It is unsurprising that Letheringham Watermill is also reputedly haunted, not by the murderer but by at least one of the victims. The place where John Bullard snr is believed to be buried is now marked by a sign which was requested by his ghost! The present mill was built around 1740 and is available to let as holiday accommodation.

The Murder of Henry Scarle

Henry Scarle worked for Mathias Kerrison, a successful businessman who owned the navigation rights to the River Waveney at Bungay Staithe. Scarle witnessed two men stealing corn from a wherry one night and informed his employer of the theft. The culprits appear to have been tipped off and savagely attacked the young man at Whitacre Burgh on the night of 10 February 1787. They then threw his body into the river, though whether he was already dead or subsequently drowned is uncertain. Henry's body was found floating face down a few days

Bungay Staithe.

later by James Black, who passed it on to Mathias Kerrison. Though one of the town's richest men, Kerrison decided to exhibit his late employee's battered corpse at Bungay's Three Tuns Inn and charged inquisitive members of the public a penny each to view it! By all accounts it was a shocking spectacle. In addition to the injuries inflicted by his attackers, the river had also taken its toll and Scarle's body was hideously bloated and virtually unrecognisable.

Thomas Mayhew and William Hawke, from Bungay and Beccles respectively, were found guilty of Henry Scarle's murder and were hanged at Castle Hill in Norwich in March 1787. Scarle lies buried in the churchyard of Holy Trinity Church, not far from St Mary's Church which is pivotal to the Black Dog of

Henry Scarle's grave, Holy Trinity Church, Bungay.

Holy Trinity Church, Bungay.

Bungay tale. Mathias Kerrison is said to have paid for the funeral and headstone from the money raised from exhibiting his body. According to the inscription the ill-fated Henry 'was valued when alive, and respected now dead'. He was just twenty-three years old.

After the indignity of being posthumously exhibited at the Three Tuns, hopefully poor Henry is not one of the many lost souls said to still inhabit the old inn (*see* chapter 'Haunted Hostelries').

Suffolk Witchcraft Trials

The belief in witchcraft was widespread for hundreds of years and Suffolk was far from unique in persecuting and executing alleged practitioners. So called 'swimming', whereby the accused was lowered into a pool or river with a rope around their neck and their hands and feet bound, was a favourite way of deciding if they were guilty or innocent. If they drowned they were pronounced innocent but if they floated they were guilty of witchcraft and usually condemned to death. Numerous towns and villages across the county had 'witch pools', including secluded Polstead, which would later become internationally known for the gruesome murder which took place there in 1827 (*see* chapter 'Maria Marten and the Red Barn Murder'). Sometimes there was no proper trial, but even if there was, the accused was often convicted on flimsy or fabricated evidence. In Suffolk, convicted witches were almost always hanged.

Older women, particularly those who lived alone and kept black cats, small dogs, birds, or other little animals as pets or companions, were most likely to be accused and convicted of witchcraft. Known as 'familiars', these were believed to be supernatural spirits that took the form of common creatures and helped the witch with her spells and potions. However, quite a lot of younger women

Witch 'swimming' took place at Polstead.

Witches Apprehended, Ex
amined and Executed, for notable
villanies by them committed both by
Land and Water.

With a strange and most true triall how to know
whether a woman be a Witch
or not.

Printed at London for *Edward Marchant*, and are to
be sold at his shop ouer against the Crosse in Pauls

Title page of 'Witches Apprehended...' 1613. (Courtesy of the Wellcome Collection CC BY-4.0) and some men were also executed as witches. A bizarre case at Denham, situated between Newmarket and Bury St Edmunds, involved a sixteen-year-old girl who was believed by the women of the village to be a witch simply because she was unusually beautiful. They complained that she had bewitched their menfolk, many of whom were besotted with her. The girl was imprisoned in St Mary's Church before being subjected to the 'swimming' test. She was bound in chains and thrown into a well, which unsurprisingly resulted in her drowning. Despite subsequently being declared innocent, she was denied a Christian burial in the churchyard and was placed in an unmarked grave beside a crossroads. The incident is said to have happened during the 1640s but the girl's name is unknown. According to a local tale her shackled skeleton was found when the road was later dug up and her remains were reburied in a graveyard, though further information is lacking. It is claimed that the rattling of chains and unexplained lights have been reported in the area.

The notorious and much-feared Matthew Hopkins, the self-styled 'Witchfinder General', was only active between around 1644 and 1646 during the English Civil War, but was responsible for many deaths across East Anglia. Estimates of the number of alleged witches executed as a result of Hopkins' activities range from around 100 to more than 400. Matthew Hopkins was the fourth son of James Hopkins, rector of Great Wenham in Suffolk. He was born in or around 1620 and began his witch-hunts in the spring of 1644 with his associate John Sterne. They travelled from town to town, hiring out their services and by all accounts making a very good living. They are believed to have used torture and sleep deprivation while interrogating their victims. Hopkins is said to have 'swum' suspected witches at various locations in Suffolk, including Framlingham Castle, now immortalised by local singer-songwriter Ed Sheran in his song *Castle on the Hill*. Witch 'swimming' was outlawed by the end of 1645 and opposition to Hopkins and Sterne was steadily growing before the pair 'retired' from witch-hunting in late 1646 or early 1647.

Hopkins is believed to have died from tuberculosis in Manningtree, Essex, on 12 August 1647, aged around twenty-seven. He was buried later that same day in an unmarked grave in St Mary's churchyard on Mistley Heath. The church no longer exists and the exact location of the Witchfinder's grave is disputed. Legend has it that Hopkins was actually 'swum' as a witch himself, and either drowned or survived the ordeal and was subsequently hanged. A variation on this theme claims that he was 'hacked to death' by a mob. There is no evidence to support such tales and it was probably wishful thinking on the part of those who demanded retribution for his crimes. In his book *The Discovery of Witches*, first published in the year of his death, Hopkins disclosed a number of dubious methods of extracting confessions. Some of his techniques were copied on the other side of the Atlantic during the New England witch-hunts of 1648–63 and the Salem Witch Trials in Massachusetts

MATTHEW HOPKINS,

OF MANNINGTREE, ESSEX,

THE CELEBRATED WITCH-FINDER.

FROM A VERY RARE PRINT IN THE PEPYSIAN LIBRARY, AT
MAGDALENE COLLEGE, CAMBRIDGE.

Matthew Hopkins, Witchfinder. (Courtesy of the Wellcome Collection CC BY-4.0)

during 1692–93. *Witchfinder General*, a controversial and very violent film loosely based on Hopkins' exploits, was released in 1968. It starred Vincent Price in the title role and was filmed in Suffolk.

A widow named Mary Lackland (or Lakeland) from Ipswich was accused of using witchcraft to kill various people including her husband John, a barber-surgeon. Other alleged victims were Henry Reade – whose ship she was supposed to have cast adrift – her grandchild's teacher John Beales, a servant called Sarah Clarke, and Elizabeth Aldham. These crimes were apparently carried out with assistance from her 'familiars' – two dogs and a mole. Mary Lackland was found guilty at her trial in Ipswich but unlike most convicted Suffolk witches she was burned at the stake in September 1645.

The seaside town once home to the 'Lowestoft Witches'.

Eighteen other convicted witches were hanged in Bury St Edmunds in 1645, after the largest single trial of its type in England. Among those executed was John Lowes, minister of Brandeston, near Framlingham, who was around eighty years old. He was found guilty of various acts of witchcraft including bewitching livestock and conjuring bad weather with the intent to cause shipwrecks. Lowes eventually confessed after being deprived of sleep for several days in addition to being 'swum' at Framlingham Castle. Others hanged included Prissilla Collit and Susanna Smith, who were both accused of infanticide in addition to witchcraft, and Susanna Stegold, who was alleged to have used witchcraft to kill her violent and abusive husband.

Nearly twenty years later, two elderly widows were also tried and convicted at Bury St Edmunds Assizes. They were Amy Denny (or Duny) and Rose Cullender, known as the 'Lowestoft Witches'. According to a copy of the trial

The Beacon or Witches' Stones, Belle Vue Park, Lowestoft.

report published in 1682, the court case took place on 10 March 1664 but other sources give the year as either 1662 or 1665. Amy Denny was said to have bewitched two daughters of Samuel Pacy, a Lowestoft fish merchant who had repeatedly refused to serve her due to rumours that she was a witch. The girls suffered severe fits and allegedly expelled many pins and a nail from their mouths. They claimed that Denny and Cullender magically materialised and tormented them, making threats and urging them to kill themselves. Three other girls came forward to claim that the two women had also bewitched them, and a woman named Dorothy Durrant accused Denny of killing her ten-year-old daughter by means of witchcraft. Various other claims were made in court and even Thomas Browne, the eminent Norwich-based doctor and author who was knighted by Charles II in 1671, stated that he believed the girls had been bewitched. Almost inevitably, Amy Denny and Rose Cullender were quickly found guilty and were hanged on 17 March.

Amy Denny is also connected with the Beacon Stones or Witches' Stones which stand in Belle Vue Park, Lowestoft, between Cart Score and the Ravine, along with an old anchor. According to local folklore she used to sit on the stones and verbally abuse people walking by. They originally formed the base of a clifftop warning beacon built on the orders of the Marquis of Northampton in 1550. Rain is said to fall if water is poured over the stones and another tale claims that they run down to the sea at midnight.

Church and Churchyard Tales

The Earthbound Bells of East Bergholt

St Mary's Church, East Bergholt, in the heart of Constable Country, is famous for its bell cage in the churchyard housing what is claimed to be the heaviest set of working bells in England. According to a local legend, work started on a church tower but every night the Devil reduced the previous day's work to rubble and the workers had to start again from scratch each morning. Eventually, after several years of this anti-social behaviour, the workers finally got the message and abandoned the tower.

The known facts are that work commenced on a bell tower in 1525 under the patronage of Cardinal Wolsey, but funds dried up and his death in 1530 signalled the end of the project. Instead it was decided to build a large wooden bell cage next to the church in 1531 to contain five bells together weighing in at 4.25 tons. One is dated 1450 and they are still rung by hand. The bells are mounted upside down in the cage, which was originally located in a different part of the churchyard. It is said that during the seventeenth century the occupant of East Bergholt Old Hall found the noise level unbearable and paid for the bell cage to be moved to the other side of the church, a position that it still occupies today.

The Bellcage, East Bergholt Church.

A 'Cracked' Church and a White Lady

As well as being one of the most remote churches in Suffolk, St Andrew's at Covehithe is also highly unusual, mainly because it nestles within the ruins of its much larger predecessor. The original church, including the present tower, was constructed during the fourteenth and fifteenth centuries but its massive scale was impractical and maintenance costs prohibitive. Permission was granted in 1672 for the church to be partly demolished and for a much smaller building to be built within its outer walls against the existing oversized tower. Some materials from the old church were recycled in the building of the new one, but much was left in place and there it remains to this day. In his *Timpson's Travels in East Anglia*, the late author and broadcaster John Timpson likened it to 'a chicken inside a cracked egg'.

The tiny hamlet of Covehithe is located between Lowestoft and Southwold, and extensive erosion of the coastline over the centuries has left the church a great deal closer to the cliff edge than it once was. It used to be 3 miles from the sea but is now less than half a mile. The road that it stands on now goes nowhere, though the church itself is not in imminent danger of toppling over the edge.

In his *Paranormal Suffolk* (Amberley Publishing, 2009), author Christopher Reeve writes that the churchyard is haunted by a frightening phantom known locally as the White Lady. Those unfortunate enough to have had close encounters with her after dark report that she is faceless! However, she does not seem to have troubled a television crew filming scenes in the churchyard for a mini-series adaptation of the P. D. James story *Death in Holy Orders*, first shown in 2003. As with many similar tales, no further information is known about Covehithe's mysterious White Lady.

Covehithe Church.

Covehithe Church.

The Wenhaston 'Doom'

The unassuming parish church in the village of Wenhaston, near Halesworth, contains a rare treasure thought to date from around 1480–1520. The story goes that a plain whitewashed wooden panel was removed from the chancel arch while renovation work was carried out inside the church in 1892. It was thought to be of no value and was left out in the open at the mercy of the elements. A shock was in store for the workmen when, following rainfall, they discovered that the whitewash had almost miraculously vanished and a graphic medieval vision of damnation and salvation had been revealed! The painting, known as the 'Doom', is a no-holds-barred warning of what may lie in store on the Day of Judgement. It tapped into the beliefs and superstitions of the time and is thought to be the work of a monk at Blythburgh Priory. The explicit scenes on the right-hand side include unclothed sinners being herded into Hell by hideous demons. The left-hand side shows the equally naked righteous entering Heaven. Hovering above them all are Jesus Christ, his mother Mary and John the Baptist.

The painting was whitewashed by puritans in the mid-sixteenth century along with similar artwork in other churches across the country. After its rediscovery centuries later, the Wenhaston 'Doom' resumed its rightful position and is a thought-provoking and still powerful snapshot of medieval hopes and fears. When I first visited the church specifically to view the 'Doom' at close quarters, it was a slightly eerie experience in the silent and

The 'Doom', Wenhaston Church.

empty building. On a second visit over a decade later, I arrived to find a large group of senior citizens happily eating their lunch beneath the apocalyptic images. It is considered to be the best surviving work of its type in England, but is only on view now because Victorian workmen left an old whitewashed piece of wood out in the rain.

The Tattingstone Wonder

A well-known building in Suffolk at first sight appears to be a little rural church, but look closer and all is not as it seems. The Tattingstone Wonder, situated to the south of Ipswich, started life as two conventional adjoining cottages. A local squire, Edward White of Tattingstone Place, owned the cottages but their dull appearance offended him as he looked out across his parkland. In or around 1790, he decided to build a third cottage on the end plus a three-sided dummy tower to produce a more interesting church-like structure. The final touch was to add a flint façade to the north face of the cottages to match the tower. The end result was a remarkable transformation which from his home looked very much like a small country church. The rear of the cottages was left unchanged – apart

The Tattingstone Wonder. (Photo © Roger Jones - geograph.org.uk - CC-BY-SA/2.0)

from the walls of the fake tower attached to the roof of the newest one! The whole building is now a single private house and is not open to the public.

Squire White is said to have remarked, 'People often wondered at nothing so I gave them something to wonder about.' 230 years later, some continue to wonder. There is no evidence that he borrowed the idea from Euston Watermill, located in the grounds of Euston Hall south-east of Thetford, but there are similarities between the two buildings. The watermill was originally constructed during the 1670s and rebuilt in the style of a church complete with tower in 1731 to provide a more interesting view and a talking point for Charles, 2nd Duke of Grafton, and his guests.

Other Curiosities

St Mary's Church in Bungay and Holy Trinity Church, Blythburgh, both have starring roles in the Black Dog of Bungay legend but also have other curious stories to tell. In addition to its allegedly haunted priory ruins, St Mary's churchyard holds the so-called Druid Stone or Devil's Stone. It is an embedded granite erratic rumoured to have been used during ancient pagan rituals, but may simply have been a direction indicator originally located at Bungay Castle. Some say that if you either dance or walk around it seven (or twelve) times, Satan

The Druid Stone, St Mary's Church, Bungay.

himself will appear! The magical stone is also capable of answering any question you dare to ask it. This involves tapping it twelve times before placing your ear to the stone to hear the reply, which may result in strange looks and unwanted answers from passers-by. The church is said to stand on a major ley line but is no longer used for worship.

Blythburgh Church, known locally as the Cathedral of the Marshes, is still without its spire as this was toppled during the terrible thunderstorm of 4 August 1577 and never rebuilt. The building's stained-glass windows were smashed along with other treasures during the Reformation, and Cromwell's army stabled its horses inside. It was a virtual ruin before being restored in the late nineteenth century, but still contains an impressive Jack o' the Clock figure made in 1682. It was once positioned on a ladder in the tower arch and tolled away the passing time, but now stands close to the organ and signals the beginning of a service. A cheery inscription warned, 'As the hours pass away, so doth the life of man decay.'

An even older Jack o' the Clock figure can be seen in St Edmund's Church, Southwold. Taking the form of a War of the Roses soldier and dating from the late fifteenth century, Southwold Jack stands around 4 feet 6 inches (1.37 metres) tall. In its left hand the figure brandishes a sword, while its right hand clasps an

Two 'Jacks' (*above*: Holy Trinity Church, Blythburgh; *below*: St Edmund's Church, Southwold).

axe which it uses to strike a bell. Like its Blythburgh counterpart, it originally tolled away the hours but now rings the bell at the start of services. Southwold Jack has been adopted as a trademark of Adnam's Brewery based in the town.

An interesting story lies behind an elaborate memorial monument to Princess Caroline Murat and her second husband in a quiet rural churchyard. The monument at All Saints' Church, Ringsfield, situated between Beccles and Bungay, features three angels and was commissioned by the couple's two daughters. The princess was not only a granddaughter of Joachim Murat, King of Naples, but also the great-niece of Emperor Napoleon Bonaparte. She was born on 31 December 1832 in Bordentown, New Jersey, USA, and married Baron Charles Martin de Chassiron in Paris in 1850. After his death, she married John Lewis Garden of Redisham Hall near Ringsfield in 1872. Garden died in 1892 and Princess Caroline passed away at Redisham Hall on 23 July 1902. Her remains were interred in the family vault after the funeral service at All Saints' Church.

Ringsfield churchyard also has a large memorial monument to Sir Nicholas Garneys, who was High Sheriff of Suffolk in 1592 and died in 1599. Instead of angels, his monument unexpectedly features a prominent figure of a mermaid (*see* photo page 21).

Princess Caroline Murat's memorial, Ringsfield Church.

Haunted Hostelries

Suffolk, in common with most other British counties, has many public houses, inns and hotels that are reputedly haunted. Some of these spooky tales are retold below.

The Three Tuns in Bungay town centre is claimed to be haunted by the restless spirit of Rex Bacon (or Hacon), who is said to have killed his wife and her lover before hanging himself in the pub. This supposedly happened in 1682 when he was just eighteen years old, though there appears to be no documented evidence of the murders or his suicide. Nevertheless, the apparition of a man hanging from a rope on the staircase has been reported along with other unexplained activity. Paranormal investigators claim to have contacted Rex Bacon and many other phantoms in the building, and the names and dates were mainly obtained during séances. A highwayman called Tom Hardy, a contemporary and possible associate

The King's Head Hotel and Three Tuns Inn, Bungay.

The Swan Hotel, Lavenham.

of Dick Turpin, was hanged for his crimes. In life Hardy often visited the Three Tuns and in death he may still frequent the old inn. Lizzie Bowlynge, a servant who was chained up and starved to death in the cellar in 1589 for the crime of stealing ale, is also reputed to be one of the resident ghosts. The aforementioned Dick Turpin and author Charles Dickens are believed to have stayed overnight at the Three Tuns.

Just across the road from the Three Tuns is the King's Head Hotel, which is also said to harbour echoes of the past. One room is claimed to be colder than the others and to have a strange and sometimes disturbing atmosphere. It has been suggested that one or more of the Three Tuns' ghosts may have made the short trip to the King's Head!

The picture-postcard village of Lavenham is famous for its ancient timbered buildings and is firmly on the Suffolk tourist map. If legend is to be believed it also has a darker side. The ghost of a woman is said to frequent a room in The Swan Hotel, after hanging herself there. According to one version she was a former employee who took the drastic action after failing to achieve a much-desired promotion. An alternative and perhaps more likely scenario is that she ended her life during the nineteenth century after falling pregnant out of wedlock and then being jilted at the altar. Also in Lavenham, the Angel Hotel is said to still be home to the spirit of one-time landlady Mrs Goodhew.

Ipswich is notable for a number of haunted hostelries. Guests who stayed in a certain bedroom at the former Neptune Inn complained of sleepless nights due to an old sailor who sat on their bed and spoke gibberish. The legend goes that a seaman called Fred was found guilty of smuggling and hanged in the courtyard during the seventeenth century. The building is now a private residence and Fred is still reputed to make nocturnal visits and natter away to himself. Also in Ipswich, the spirit of a young child has been reported at the Lord Nelson, while a female ghost has been seen to pass through a solid wall at the Great White Horse Hotel. A woman is believed to have been killed in a fire there during the 1920s. The Halberd Inn is reputedly haunted by a murdered monk whose body was put down an indoor well, while the Woolpack may harbour several ghosts. These include Admiral Edward Vernon – known as 'Old Grog' after passing a law to add water to rum rations on naval vessels – along with a one-time owner of the pub and a monk.

The White Hart Inn, Blythburgh, already mentioned in connection with smuggling and the story of convicted murderer Tobias Gill, may also have a resident ghost. In her *Haunted East Anglia* (1974), author Joan Forman tells of occasional unexplained knocking on an old oak door behind the bar, as if made by someone wearing a ring. The building was previously an Ecclesiastical Court House and the noises could be an echo from a time when priests or priors regularly wore rings. The former Blythburgh Priory, which is also claimed to be haunted, is situated on the opposite side of the road from the White Hart.

The former Anchor Hotel (later known as Bayfields) in Lowestoft's High Street was said to be haunted by a hooded monk-like figure that was seen intermittently over many years. During the Second World War, a sailor's sleep was interrupted by a cold blast of air and he awoke to briefly see the apparition before it suddenly vanished. Similar sightings were claimed in the hotel in 1976 and the figure has also been reported in the general locality. At the time of writing the building has been closed for several years.

According to legend a young serving maid had a short-lived affair with Edward Montague, Earl of Sandwich, on the eve of the Battle of Sole Bay in 1672. When he was killed in action the girl was broken-hearted and died a short time later. She is said to still frequent a bedroom in Sutherland House, a hotel and restaurant in Southwold High Street.

Charms of various sorts were often placed in buildings to help protect against witchcraft, evil spirits and bad luck. Mummified cats were sometimes bricked

Sutherland House, Southwold.

The Mill Hotel, Sudbury. (Photo courtesy of Rosalind Middleton)

up and one of these unfortunate creatures was discovered when the old Sudbury Watermill was converted to a hotel in the 1970s. It is now on display in the foyer but was once sold to a local shop which burned down soon after. During the time it was away, the Mill Hotel is said to have also experienced bad luck including flooding and other problems. After somehow surviving the fire, the mummified moggy was returned to its rightful home and order was restored. Nevertheless, the older part of the hotel is rumoured to be haunted by the ghost of a woman who met a grisly end beneath the waterwheel when the building was still a working mill.

Another mummified cat hangs above the bar of The Nutshell in Bury St Edmunds, which is officially Britain's smallest public house. The cat is said to be cursed and anyone who touches it can expect bad luck to befall them. Thieves and pranksters who removed it from the pub quickly returned it after apparently falling victim to the 'curse'. An apparition of a young boy believed to be a murder victim has been seen on the top floor and a phantom monk also haunts the building. The Nutshell is on the site of an earlier building where those accused of witchcraft were interrogated.

The Angel Hotel, Bury St Edmunds.

Also in Bury St Edmunds, the area around Angel Hill and the priory ruins is said to be a hotspot of paranormal activity. Various sightings have been claimed including yet more ghostly monks and a Grey Lady who appears in the churchyard of St Edmundsbury Cathedral at 11 p.m. on 24 February. The Angel Hotel, built in 1778 on the site of a fifteenth-century coaching inn, has cellars dating back another 200 years. According to some it has a haunted underground bar where unexplained nocturnal footsteps have been heard. Charles Dickens stayed at the Angel Hotel in 1835, 1859 and 1861, and his old room (formerly No. 11 but now renumbered 215) is inevitably now called the Charles Dickens Suite. The superstar author wrote *The Pickwick Papers* there but, slightly inconveniently, there seems to be no suggestion that he still visits his old room.

Modern Tales: Atomic Bombs, UFOs and a 'Timeslip'

Although some of these 'modern' stories are now rapidly disappearing into the mists of time, compared with most of the old tales included in this book they are still very recent history. From top-secret weapons tests and a major UFO incident at a military base, to an alleged failed wartime invasion and an unexplained 'out of time' experience, the events explored below add a new twist to the rich heritage of Suffolk folklore. It is interesting that several of the incidents took place within a small 'Suffolk Triangle' between Woodbridge, Shingle Street and Orford Ness!

The Secrets of Orford Ness

The narrow spit of shingle known as Orford Ness, separated from the village of Orford by the River Alde, has a strange and mysterious recent history. During the First World War, German prisoners were held at the remote location and the testing of prototype aircraft, parachutes, and camouflage techniques also took place there. A special radio beacon was erected in 1929 and radar was developed during the following decade. In the late 1960s and early 1970s, a highly advanced radar system codenamed Cobra Mist was developed in partnership with the US military. Atomic bomb tests were carried out at Orford Ness from the 1950s onwards and 'pagodas' with massive reinforced walls and roofs were built. According to official records, the bomb casings and detonators were tested but no nuclear material was ever used.

Of course, all of these clandestine operations were classified as 'Top Secret' at the time, and even now the full extent of what happened at Orford Ness can only be guessed at. This has inevitably led to various conspiracy theories, not least that fully armed nuclear weapons testing may have taken place. Another rumour links the site with captured alien craft and strange lights have been reported.

For decades the facility at Orford Ness was one of the most closely guarded in Britain, but was decommissioned in 1983. The area is now a National Nature Reserve and is open to the public. The famous Orfordness Lighthouse was built in 1792 and worked until June 2013. Though not part of the military facility, it became embroiled in another conspiracy theory due to claims that it may have been the source of mysterious lights seen in Rendlesham Forest in 1980. That story is examined in detail later. A bungalow beside the lighthouse finally collapsed in late September 2019 after being battered by high waves and strong

Abandoned buildings at Orford Ness.

winds. It was sadly announced in February 2020 that the lighthouse itself would shortly be dismantled before it succumbed to the sea. The building of a shorter replica further inland has been proposed.

Strange Happenings at Shingle Street

One of the strangest stories of the Second World War relates to an alleged Nazi invasion attempt at Shingle Street, south of Orford Ness. This supposedly happened on the evening and night of 31 August 1940, and resulted in many burned bodies being washed ashore. Legend has it that they were part of an enemy landing party but the British got wind of the planned invasion and somehow set the sea alight. The bodies were said to be wearing German uniforms and were later loaded onto British Army trucks and driven away. All those who took part in or witnessed the incident were ordered never to say a word about it. It seems that most obeyed, at least in public, and it wasn't until the 1990s that the story really started to gain momentum. Since then a few people have come forward claiming to be eyewitnesses, along with relatives of those who have now died. Probably the most high-profile alleged eyewitness was the late Ronald Ashford, who passed away in December 2013. He insisted to the end of his life that the events described above were true and campaigned on his website for the publication of

Orfordness Lighthouse.

all information relating to the case. Some declassified papers were released into the public domain in 1993, but made no mention of an invasion attempt. Other documents are due to be made public in 2021. Conspiracy theories abound but some historians dismiss claims of a failed German landing at Shingle Street as fantasy and propaganda.

UFO Sightings in Rendlesham Forest

This is one of Suffolk's newer tales but it has quickly found a unique place in the county's folklore. Some UFO investigators claim that aliens landed in Rendlesham Forest near Woodbridge in late December 1980 and that the incident ranks as 'Britain's Roswell' (after the site of an alleged alien spacecraft crash in New Mexico, USA, in 1947).

Reports of strange lights in the forest were investigated by servicemen from the United States Air Force base on the former RAF Bentwaters site, in the early hours of Boxing Day, 1980. The lights returned around forty-eight hours later on the early morning of 28 December and again troops were scrambled. Lieutenant Colonel Charles Halt, the deputy commander at the airbase, was with his men and made an audio recording of the incident on cassette tape. The recording was made public in 1984 and Halt can be heard giving a running commentary

Above and below: Rendlesham Forest.

of events including sightings of flashing lights through the forest. The lights continued to be seen intermittently for some time but remained unidentified. It was later reported that a serviceman, Sergeant Jim Penniston, claimed to have seen and even touched what he believed to have been a craft of extraterrestrial origin in Rendlesham Forest that night. Penniston's original statement contained no reference to any such object being found. Another unsubstantiated account alleges that two US Air Force personnel followed an unidentified hovering craft from a distance of around 50 yards (45.7 metres) before it suddenly vanished. Radiation readings were taken and levels were found to be higher in some areas of the forest than in others.

So what, if anything, really happened in Rendlesham Forest at the end of 1980? In a signed affidavit nearly thirty years later in June 2010, Lieutenant Colonel Halt accused both the American and British authorities of burying evidence of an extraterrestrial encounter, though, like Penniston, he appeared to contradict some elements of his original account. Many theories have been put forward over the years including the possibility that the flashing light was simply the beacon of Orfordness Lighthouse a few miles away. Though some UFO investigators scoff at this suggestion, claiming that the lighthouse was well known to the Americans, some of the eyewitnesses compared the flashing lights to a lighthouse beacon. Halt himself said on the now famous tape that the flashes occurred every five seconds, which coincided with the flash cycle of Orfordness Lighthouse. Officers from Suffolk Police who also investigated the incident reported seeing only the repetitive flashing light of the lighthouse.

A fireball reported over quite a large area of southern England early on 26 December 1980 may have been the source of the original sighting at Rendlesham. Various accusations of deliberate hoaxes have also been made over the last four decades. A few years ago, a local farmer came forward to claim that he had been working on the nights in question and that the lights were probably from his machinery as he crisscrossed his fields. He suggested that when viewed through the trees in the forest they could have been mistaken for something more sinister. This explanation was also firmly rejected by UFO investigators. As with the notorious Roswell incident, the events in Rendlesham Forest remain the subject of numerous conspiracy theories and the truth will probably never be known. Parts of the forest were obliterated by the great storm of October 1987, but a so-called 'UFO Trail' was opened to the public in 2005. An artist's interpretation of a craft described in some accounts was unveiled there in 2014.

More Close Encounters of the Suffolk Kind

Twenty-seven years before the Rendlesham Forest incident, John Smith, a member of the Royal Observer Corps, reported seeing a UFO near Kessingland. He described it as being 'discus shaped with a diameter of around 50 feet (15.2 metres)' and with 'four large orangey rays' shining from its dome. He was skilled in aircraft recognition and was convinced that it was an unknown type of craft.

The sighting took place in October 1953 and a similar object was reported over Norwich later the same evening, witnessed by a number of people. Other UFO sightings in the Kessingland area were claimed in 1995 and 2009.

Strange sightings have also been made at Hollesley, just north of Shingle Street and slightly south of Orford Ness. A large, dark-coloured, triangular-shaped craft was reported by villages in late October 1983. Three bright lights were visible on the base of the object as it hovered for around fifteen minutes. According to contemporary press reports, some onlookers said the object was completely silent while at least one said it emitted 'a high-pitched whine'. Nearby RAF Woodbridge stated that nothing was detected by radar and made no further comment. Some believe that the villages saw a top-secret prototype of the B-2 Spirit stealth bomber, which appears to fit the general description and may have been undergoing test flights in the area around that time. This and other experimental aircraft could also account for other UFO sightings.

Hollesley village sign. (Photo © Adrian Cable - geograph.org.uk - CC-BY-SA/2.0)

Another UFO incident over Hollesley, this time with a weird twist, was claimed as recently as 31 August 2017. An anonymous witness stated that she and her daughter 'saw a flash line of bright white light' as they were driving home at around 11 p.m. The lights kept disappearing and reappearing as they drove past Hollesley Bay Prison and towards Bawdsey. After the woman turned the car around to get a closer look, they then saw another ball of light and suddenly found themselves outside a shop in Hollesley. The driver claimed that it would have taken them at least ten minutes to arrive in the village from their previous location, yet the journey took just seconds. In a statement to the British Earth and Aerial Mysteries Society (BEAMS) she remarked, 'it was as though we'd just been teleported from one place to another!'

The Kersey 'Timeslip' Mystery

Three fifteen-year-old Royal Navy cadets were on a map-reading exercise one fine Sunday morning in October 1957, which would lead them to the picturesque village of Kersey near Hadleigh. As they approached they heard church bells ringing, but on entering Kersey the atmosphere became increasingly oppressive and unpleasant. There was not a breath of wind or any birdsong, and the whole village was silent and seemingly deserted. There were a few ducks around the stream which crosses the narrow main street, but even they were eerily quiet and made no movement. The youths were taken aback at the apparent strangeness of the place and stopped to peer through the window of a building. Inside they saw two or three skinned oxen carcasses, which they later described as being 'mouldy green'. They assumed that the place was a butcher's shop which seemed to have been suddenly abandoned. The troubled trio also looked through the grimy window of another house and found it to be empty with not a stick of furniture.

At this point the lads felt the urge to get out of the village straight away and did not look back until they reached the top of a hill overlooking it. Turning round, they saw that smoke was now rising from chimneys – which they swore was not the case moments before – and could again hear the church bells ringing. They could also see the church tower, which for some reason they were unable to make out earlier. The cadets wasted no further time in reporting back to their superiors, who unsurprisingly did not take their descriptions of an abandoned 'medieval' village seriously.

Around thirty years later, one of the former cadets wrote a letter to author Andrew MacKenzie, of the Society for Psychical Research, in which he gave his personal account of what happened that autumn morning in deepest Suffolk. William Laing, originally from Perthshire in Scotland, had emigrated to Australia but had never forgotten his strange experience in Suffolk. He later revisited Kersey, together with Andrew MacKenzie, in 1990. The house Laing identified as the butcher's shop was a private residence and had been since well before 1957. However, records showed that it was built around 1350 and had been used as a butcher's shop in 1790 and possibly earlier. William Laing claimed that on his

Above and below: Kersey village.

previous visit he 'experienced an overwhelming feeling of sadness and depression' and 'also a feeling of unfriendliness and unseen watchers...'

Andrew Mackenzie also contacted the other two witnesses – Michael Crowley, from Worcestershire, and Londoner Ray Baker. Crowley, who had also moved to Australia and had remained in contact with Laing, corroborated much of the Scotsman's account though not in as much detail. Baker, however, could not recall anything odd happening in the village. Mackenzie included the case in his book *Adventures in Time* (1997) and believed that the cadets may have encountered a 'timeslip', where people somehow experience a place as it was at some point in the past. His research revealed that when the Black Death was at its height in England (around 1348–49) and many communities were evacuated, Kersey Church was unfinished and without a tower.

Could the teenagers really have gone back in time or did they simply get disorientated in unfamiliar surroundings? None were local and would never have seen a village like Kersey before. Many years later, William Laing spoke of a 'ghost village' and the absence of cars, telephone lines and television aerials, but that could also be said of many other rural locations in the 1950s. Even today, entering the beautiful village of Kersey is like stepping back in time and for that very reason it is highly popular with tourists and film-makers alike. Of course, this does not explain the 'abandoned' houses or the 'phantom' butcher's shop with its rotting carcasses – unless the three cadets unwittingly stumbled upon a film set that Sunday morning in 1957?

Bibliography

Brooks, Pamela, *Suffolk Ghosts and Legends: Scandals, Sieges and Spooks* (Wellington: Halsgrove, 2009)

Haining, Peter, *Maria Marten: The Murder in the Red Barn* (Plymouth: Images, 1992)

Haining, Peter, *The Supernatural Coast: Unexplained Mysteries of East Anglia* (London: Robert Hale Ltd, 1992)

Jeffery, Peter, *East Anglian Ghosts, Legends and Lore* (Gillingham: The Old Orchard Press, 1988)

Jennings, Pete, *Haunted Suffolk* (Stroud: Tempus Publishing Ltd, 2006)

Mills West, Harold, *East Anglia Tales of Mystery & Murder* (Newbury, Countryside Books, 1996)

Mower, Mark, *Suffolk Tales of Mystery & Murder* (Newbury, Countryside Books, 2006)

O'Brien, Rick, *East Anglian Curiosities* (Wimborne: The Dovecote Press Ltd, 1992)

Reeve, Christopher, *The Black Dog of Bungay* (pamphlet, 1988)

Reeve, Christopher, *Paranormal Suffolk* (Stroud, Amberley Publishing, 2009)

Timpson, John, *Timpson's Travels in East Anglia* (London: William Heinemann Ltd, 1990)